CREATION IN CRISIS
Responding to God's Covenant

Shantilal P. Bhagat

BRETHREN PRESS
Elgin, Illinois

Creation in Crisis:Responding to God's Covenant

Shantilal P. Bhagat

Cover design by Jeane Healy
Cover photo © Robert Cushman Hayes, All Rights Reserved

Library of Congress Cataloguing-in-Publication Data
Bhagat, Shantilal P., 1923-
Creation in crisis: responding to God's covenant/Shantilal P.
  Bhagat.
  p.cm.
Includes bibliographical references.
ISBN 0-87178-164-6 (pbk.)
  1. Human ecology—Religious aspects—Christianity. 2. Na-
  ture—Religious aspects—Christianity. I. Title.
BT695.5.B534 1990   261.8'3628—dc20   90-45512
                                                        CIP

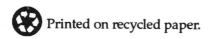 Printed on recycled paper.

Manufactured in the United States of America

Contents

PART I. A Christian Understanding of Creation

PART II. Planet Earth

PART III. Human Degradation of Creation

PART IV. Other Factors Impacting the Creation

PART V. Economy and Ecology Linkages

PART VI. The Human Future

Appendices

ACKNOWLEDGMENTS

The inspiration to write this book has come from a variety of sources and I owe a debt to all of them. The idea to prepare a study resource that could provide a comprehensive overview to lay people in the context of their faith and beliefs originated in a consultation that I was invited to attend four years ago.

At this consultation I heard keynoters with their scholarly speeches and small groups discussing strategies for action and involvement. However, most touching for me were the real life stories presented by a number of women who had taken the initiative in their small communities—mostly ethnic minorities—to get organized for confronting large corporations that were polluting soil, air, and water and threatening, in some instances, the life and the very existence of individuals, families and communities. Their dedication, courage, zeal, and the ability to research and articulate issues made a lasting impression on me. Their repeated question—"Where is the Church as we struggle with the very basic issue of life and survival for ourselves, the Earth, and the future generations?" has never left me. In my continuing contact with some of these modern "saints" and prophets I have been nurtured in my faith and have gained insights that helped me write this book. To these men and women I owe a large debt.

I am indebted to the work of many researchers, nonprofit organizations including the Worldwatch Institute, the World Resources Institute, Friends of the Earth, the Natural Defense Council, and others. I have made extensive use of the popular press—the *New York Times* in particular to keep abreast of developments. The materials published by the United Nations provided a global perspective. I have relied on a variety of magazines for data and viewpoints. I have drawn heavily from books and publications of ecumenical organizations such as the World Council of Churches, the National Council of Churches of Christ (U.S.), and the religious press in the United States.

For their early reading and critique of my manuscript, I am indebted to Calvin DeWitt, Jaydee Hanson, Job Ebenezer, and Owen Owens—all of whom reviewed the manuscript from their

Christian faith perspective and made suggestions that helped improve the final copy of the manuscript. The able editing by Jennifer Schrock and the assistance by Linda Bohne in the preparation of the manuscript made my task manageable.

For the many opportunities for contacts at the grassroots level, at public hearings and through field visits, I am indebted to the Eco-Justice Working Group of the National Council of Churches. My special tribute goes to Chris Cowap, who as the first staff person for the Working Group, provided dynamic leadership and vision to the Group in spite of her continuing fight with a terminal health problem.

I am indebted to the Church of the Brethren General Board, the World Ministries Commission, the Administrative Council, my staff colleagues in the World Ministries Commission, and my Executive Roger Schrock for their support, understanding and encouragement which made it possible for me to write this book.

Most of all, I owe an unpayably large debt to my wife, Tsun-Hsien. She not only worked diligently to collect relevant materials from the newspapers but also supplied other assistance essential to maintaining my sanity while I completed the book. My grandchildren, Taryn and Nicholas, who were playing around me during the writing of parts of this book, constantly kept before me the question of what sort of world and the future I am leaving behind for them and million others like them who will be following me/us.

Finally, I owe the largest debt to the community of life that has made this book possible: the air, water, soil, and life of Earth, and the fire of our star, the sun. Thank you, God, for all of the above and for loving humankind in spite of their shortcomings and violence to Your Creation.

Shantilal P. Bhagat
Elgin, Illinois

FOREWORD

That joyful song of Creation, Psalm 104, teaches that the work of God brings water to beasts of the field, makes grass grow for the cattle, and gives plants for people to cultivate. It teaches that the earth is satisfied by the fruit of God's work. And our daily living confirms this truth as we walk God's fruitful Creation—reaping abundant harvests, observing productive forests and prairies, enjoying endless waves of migrating birds. God's work is *fruitful*. Creation is *fruitful*!

Yet, as Shantilal Bhagat so clearly describes in this book, we find Creation's fruitfulness being diminished and strained. Our blessed expectation that *all creatures* here below can bring God praise—expressed in our singing of the doxology—is shaken by the daily extinguishing of those very creatures that praise their Creator. In the night of many of our cities the reading of Psalm 19 does not provide the inspiration it clearly is intended to give—for how, beneath a blanket of obscuring smog, can we join with the psalmist to proclaim "The heavens declare the glory of God!" In going their own way people are impoverishing the Creation's ability to declare God's glory. In their exercise of selfish power and profligate wasting of Creation, people are making God's everlasting power and divinity (Rom. 1:20) less clearly seen. Once green with perennial vegetation, pastures of the countryside have been diminished as the cattle of a thousand hills have been removed off the land. Once quiet and still with ecological health, waters of streams and ponds have gained a disquieting turbulence as they bear their wasteful loads. Creation's evangelical testimony is increasingly smogged and muted. Creation's song of praise— its testimony—is being impoverished by insatiable, grasping hands and machines.

What must we say to this thankless usership? To this self-directed abuse of Creation? This book helps us personally to find the words to respond to this degradation of Creation. It also gives us its own response—a response that can be summarized thus: As our Creator tends us and all Creation so must we tend the Garden. As God keeps us, so must we keep the Creation (Gen. 2:15). Imaging our Sustainer, we *must* sustain Creation.

Reflecting our Redeemer, we must also reconcile *all things*. Our stewardship is so to live on Earth that Heaven will not be a shock to us!

Shantilal Bhagat here describes Creation's degradation, not for the purpose of bringing gloom to our minds, but as a challenge to ourselves and our churches to take *very seriously* our calling as stewards of Earth and its creatures. While not denying us the celebration of the fruits of God's Creation, Shantilal makes clear the biblical warning that we are not to diminish or destroy Creation's fruitfulness. His writing points each of us toward our worthy calling: to be thankful and caring *keepers* of Creation—even as we enjoy its fruitfulness. Affirming that our stewardship is one that is expected to bear fruit, he provides us with Appendices that are truly resources to help refurbish and build our stewardship of Creation. And, in his concluding call to the churches, whom he describes as "the undeveloped key to the environmental crisis," Shantilal identifies four areas where the church is called to act. The last of these summarizes them all, and in a very real sense makes it possible to respond to this book with stewardly action; it is to make each church a *Creation Awareness Center*. While giving some specific suggestions on what such a concept might involve, this entire book provides a powerful catalyst for making any particular church a Creation Awareness Center, shaped by its theology, talents, local situation and opportunities.

The vitally important message of this important book is that we must not diminish Creation's fruitfulness, but foster it. It is that Creation remains God's (Ps. 24:1), while God *trusts* us with it! It is because of this trust in us that we respond as faithful stewards. In this magnificently fruitful Creation, we are to image Creation's Sustainer, giving thanks to God and being disciples of Jesus Christ. It is as disciples of our Master Steward that our lives in Creation can be lives of stewardly service— lives of thankfulness. Thankful stewardship of Creation is our worthy calling!

Calvin B. DeWitt
Oregon, Wisconsin

1
INTRODUCTION

Humans can now get so far away from the Earth that we can see the Earth and moon as two small spheres against blackness. This perspective from the moon affirms that we are Earthlings, citizens of a wonderful cloud-swathed blue sphere, that we share with several million other life forms. But even without such photographs, events of our own making have recently reminded us that we are deep-air creatures. The cues are acid rain, a warming climate, asthma, watering eyes, strange industrial smells, and geiger counters clicking in basements.

On Earth Day 1990, more than 100 million people in 140 nations honored their common home, the Earth. With speeches and symbolic actions, they called on both political leaders and individuals to take responsibility for cleaning up the environment. It was the largest mass demonstration in our world's history and marked the 20th anniversary of the first Earth Day.

It was not a victory celebration but an event to draw attention to the sobering fact that the Earth, our only home, is on the verge of a breakdown. Measured on any scale, the world is in worse shape today than it was 20 years ago. Despite all of our accomplishments, problems compound every passing year. Environmental threats now vie with nuclear war as the preeminent peril to all life in God's Creation.

Humans and Environment

Never before has our own species wielded so much power over the created order. Over five billion humans together with our advanced technology make the human race a formidable force threatening the ecosphere and its life-giving capabilities. Moreover, today's destruction of the environment is different from all the previous ones because it is systematic, of worldwide dimensions, and faster than the natural regulating mechanisms. Since the early 1970s, reports from a variety of sources confirm these dramatic developments.

After decades of neglect, environmental issues have become mainstream political issues in many countries. "Green" parties are sprouting in most democracies. People are ready to pay attention when clear, specific programs are offered. Nations are starting to address problems like the greenhouse effect, acid rain and the thinning of the ozone shield with some of the same seriousness once reserved for international security and economic affairs. We are seeing a greening of geopolitics and the politicians are beginning to view the planet as a single ecosystem.

Twenty years after the Stockholm Conference on the Human Environment, the United Nations will hold a Conference on Environment and Development in Brazil in June 1992. There have been dramatic changes during these twenty years. First, environmental degradation is threatening survival globally, regionally and locally. This includes ozone layer depletion, the greenhouse effect, deforestation, desertification, pollution of the oceans, and the universal urban nightmare. Second, the USSR and Eastern Europe, which were absent at Stockholm, have rejoined the global community. Third, if in 1972 the ecological citizens' groups were primarily Western, there is now a blossoming environmental movement all over the South. Networks exist in Africa, Asia, and among thousands of local groups in Brazil, Colombia, Mexico, Venezuela and other countries.

Creation's Challenge to Humans

With the Decade of the Environment—the 1990s—just beginning, we who believe in the value and purpose of Creation are challenged. Because we believe the Creator has given us responsibility to be "stewards" and "caretakers," we must face squarely the problems of severe environmental degradations that surround us today. They threaten the ecosphere's future and therefore our own future.

To the Creator who has entrusted us with the responsibility of caring for Creation and to coming generations, we owe a response. Can something be done soon enough to make a difference? The crises of our times are not occasions for doomsaying pessimism nor a chance to peddle empty-hope optimism.

Every crisis is a judgment, a call to see where things have gone wrong and to seek to set matters right. The environmental crisis, the economic crisis, the crisis of faith and of militarism—are symptoms not only that humanity has not yet become what it has to be, but also that it is on the wrong track.

First of all, we need community efforts at the national and international level that will guide the interests of humanity as a whole. The church of Jesus Christ is a community set within the human community and it needs now to cut across the borders of church and world and across the confines of each separate religion or secular ideology.

Secondly, we who are part of the Christian community are challenged to seek a fresh understanding of the relationship between God, humans and the world. We need a clear vision of the role humanity plays between God and the world. For example, our nuclear capability places human beings of the late twentieth century on the verge of eliminating themselves and most if not all other forms of life on earth. In this unprecedented danger, we must ask whether the Judeo-Christian tradition's image of God as all-powerful King is helpful or harmful. Does it support human responsibility for the fate of the earth, or does it shift the burden to God? If a case can be made that the traditional imagery threatens the continuation of life, then we must give serious attention to alternatives.

Human beings are mediators, poised between two realities— God and the world. They share in both, they are united to both. They cannot live apart from either. That is the meaning of the incarnation of Jesus Christ. The only humanity that can survive is the new humanity, the humanity that has now been insepara-bly united with God in Jesus Christ. And because of its locus in the one divine-human nature of Christ, the new humanity is a mediating humanity—a humanity that reconciles human be-havior with God's caring for the world. It is an incarnate humanity—a humanity that is an inseparable part of the whole Creation and inseparably united to the Creator. Christ is iden-tified as mediator, as incarnate—the one who becomes flesh. The human presence is identified as mirrors (images) of God—of the one who sustains, cares, upholds, and keeps the Creation.

This, then, is the meaning of human presence in the cosmos. To be with one who unites. To be in Christ, bridging the divine and the human, the Creator and the Creation, the spiritual and the scientific.

Since the early 1960s, environmentalists like Rachel Carson, author of *Silent Spring*, have been alerting us to the threats our planet and life upon it face. Even though we responded with some legislation and some concern, the 1970s and 1980s have seen a worsening of environmental conditions—global warming, huge oil spills, extinction of hundreds of species, depletion of the ozone layer, pollution of our oceans, rivers and lakes, acid rain on northern woodlands, the destruction of old growth temperate forests, and now the deforestation of tropical jungles—to name a few. The dangers we now know are real!

Science and technology are important tools for solving our environmental problems—and sound legislation is also needed. But experts are beginning to understand that, by themselves, these forces alone will not avert environmental disaster.

But if the religious communities around the globe awaken to the ethical and spiritual dimensions of the environmental threat, there is hope for the Planet. It is our only hope, since it is based on our trust in the Creator. Survival is not the central issue, especially for Christians, who believe that care of Creation is a joyful, praising service and that history has to come to an end some time. For humanity the personal enemies are sin and death—death of the race, death of the planet, and personal death—or evil and loss of being. But these are precisely the enemies which have been faced and overcome by the cross and resurrection of Christ.

Christians today live to affirm and advance the opposites of sin and death—that is righteousness (justice) and life. We can face the impasse calmly and without panic, but this does not absolve us from the responsibility to join the fight against the powers of darkness and death. We have to identify these powers in a fresh way, name them, challenge them, and overcome them. Christ has, through his church, commanded us to overcome evil by good, death by life. We need not only to call evil by its name, but also to work with God to create the good. We are aware of the deadly threats which humanity is facing today. But God is God of life who will not abandon the work of God's hands. Rather, God calls us to abandon the ways of injustice, violence and exploitation. God's call for conversion is the door of life.

We give thanks to God, the Creator of all that exists; to God the Son who has reconciled the world and offers salvation to all people, individually and together; to God the Spirit, who brings life and makes perfect. We look forward to the coming reign of

God where justice and peace will embrace each other and the whole Creation will be made new. We give thanks for every sign of the reign of God manifest in our midst.

About This Book

This book attempts to integrate theological reflection about humanity's relationship to Creation with a description of the major environmental problems facing the United States and our world. A primary goal is to broaden the understanding of youth and adults in church settings about Creation, its degradation by human activities and what needs to be done to keep and heal the Creation.

The book can be used for group study, for example, in a thirteen session church school quarter. However, it is also written for persons who wish to read it on their own or for those who wish to study it in small group settings. Suggestions for reflection and group discussion are provided at the end of the chapters.

Much of this book does not make pleasant reading. It is intended to provide a comprehensive overview of our ecological ills in order to inspire action. But through it all we can continually praise God for Creation's integrity and the privilege to be part of Creation and to care for it. Therefore, a presentation of the best available data, even though it may be scary or depressing, is unavoidable.

Following the general introduction, the book begins with a biblically based understanding of Creation. It then explores the concept of nature and the history of our home, Planet Earth and its ecosystems. Several chapters go into specific degradations— the greenhouse effect, ozone depletion, air pollution, deforestation, water pollution, waste accumulation and land's misuse. Chapters on population and its impact upon the environment, biotechnology, and the interlinkages between ecology and economy provide the overall context within which we are addressing the environmental issues. The final chapter is a call to churches to give urgent attention to God's Creation in crisis and to make environmental and ecological concerns an important part of the church's ministry.

The appendices give the sources for facts and assertions not referenced in the book. They provide a sampling of reading materials and organizations, should you decide to focus more of your attention on long-term issues. A list of videos and action-oriented guides are also provided.

For Reflection and Group Discussion

1. Begin your study by inviting older members of your group to tell about changes in the environment they have witnessed in their lifetimes. How does your group feel about these changes?

2. Set up a bulletin board or file for additional information. Invite group members to clip newspaper and magazine articles on local environmental problems and what is being done about them.

3. Is concern for the earth an item of discussion or factor in decision-making at your work place? How would your boss or co-workers respond if you shared this book with them.

4. Choose a setting where you spend a significant amount of time. What environmental issues need to be addressed in that setting? What prevents people from tackling them? Work individually and then pool your lists.

5. How do you respond to the statement that —"environmental threats now vie with nuclear war as the pre-eminent peril to all life"? Which one do you worry about more? Why?

6. Ask the children in your lives to draw a picture of God, people and the world. You might help them focus their ideas by having them illustrate one of the following texts:

   Ps. 24:1-2 (the earth is the Lord's)
   Ps. 96:11-13 (trees sing for joy at God's coming)
   Gen. 1:26-31 (God's charge to humans)

   How does your group picture the God/human/world relationship? Use these drawings as a springboard for discussion.

PART I

A Christian Understanding of Creation

2
BIBLICAL
PERSPECTIVES
ON CREATION

Many chapters in this book describe the ecological impact of human beings on Planet Earth. These accounts of Creation's degradation through human activity suggest clearly that the earth is in agony and that the ecological crisis is upon us. Biocide—the destruction of life forms with their environment—is commonplace. We seem to have chosen the path of death. Yet the Bible invites us to the path of life.

The Jewish scholar Cassuto in his commentary on Genesis noted two streams of literature about Creation in the Bible. One is the prose tradition contained in Genesis 1-3. The other is the poetic tradition found in the Psalms, the Prophets, and the Wisdom literature. While there are differences between the two traditions, they do share several fundamental presuppositions.

The first common presupposition is the conviction that God in Creation ordered the world, setting boundaries and that this ordered world is a good world. Creation brought forth a cosmos from chaos (Gen.1:2). The Psalms frequently affirm that the earth was founded by God and that it declares God's glory (Ps. 19; Rom. 1:20). Seemingly unruly elements like sea will not cross their appointed boundaries, the earth will not be moved (Ps. 74:12-17).

The first assertion about the goodness of God's created world, leads to the second fundamental tenet of Israelite faith: God as Creator is sovereign over what has been created. "The world stands firm; it cannot be shaken. Your throne stands firm from of old; from eternity You have existed" (Ps. 93:1b, 2) illustrates that the two motifs run parallel to each other. The orderliness of Creation and God's lordship also go hand in hand in Psalm 74:12-17.

God as Creator entails another implication—what God created belongs to God. Psalm 24:1-2, is perhaps the most familiar passage establishing God's ownership: "The earth is the Lord's and the fullness thereof, the world and those who dwell therein; for he has founded it upon the seas, and established it upon the rivers." God's ownership of Creation is, in turn, basic to biblical concepts of justice. This is exemplified in the Jubilee legislation—laws calling for land redistribution. "But the land shall not be sold in perpetuity, for the land is mine;for you are strangers and sojourners with me. And in all the country you possess, you shall grant a redemption of the land" (Lev. 25:23-24). People may use God's land, but they do not own it.

The Bible, then, depicts God as Creator who brings about an orderliness which is good. God relates to the whole Creation as its sovereign and owner (Deut. 10:14; Ps. 24:1; 1 Cor. 10:26). Creation in turn relies upon God for its continuation and gives water and food to all creatures (Ps.104; Acts 14:17). The entire universe—not just people—speaks eloquently of the Creator (Ps. 19). God's realm includes trees; nature also praises and gives glory to God. Creation extols the glory of God (Psalms 19 and 96). We are reaffirmed that the Lord blesses us and *keeps* us (Ps. 104; Num.6:24-26).

In spite of such clear messages concerning the Creation there seems to be confusion, neglect and simple biblical ignorance among Christians. The need for fresh attention to the whole of the Bible's perspectives on the created order—the Earth, land, soil, animals, water, food ,the environment—is urgent. We are thankful for the beginning that has been made but a lot more needs to happen in order to meet the challenges now and into the future.

Let us examine some of the biblical passages and perspectives that might deepen our own understanding of God's Creation.

The Creation Story

The most obvious biblical texts for understanding the doctrine of Creation are in the first 11 chapters of the book of Genesis. These chapters are not a scientific account and are not intended to describe how the universe was made. But, they are a theological statement of the createdness and goodness of Creation and the human choice to violate that goodness (Gen. 1-11).

The doctrine of Creation as recorded in Genesis affirms three basic truths about the universe and the human race: 1. The universe did not initially bring itself into being but God brought it into being and God continues to sustain it. 2. Humankind through disobedience has violated and devastated the world in which God placed it. 3. Humans were assigned to be in a mutually sustaining relationship with one another, with the Creation, and with God.

The goodness of the Creation is understood in the first chapter of Genesis. "And God saw that it was good" are the words continually repeated after God created water, land, plants, light, fish, birds, and land animals. The completed Creation was called "very good."

All the important passages on Creation are not limited to the first three chapters of Genesis. Creation is good because it is the work of God and all parts of Creation—not just humans—are pictured as praising God's glory with thanksgiving and joy. And it is this we affirm when we sing the Doxology: "Praise God from whom all blessings flow. Praise God all creatures here below." The Psalms constantly echo the theme that the whole Creation responds to the Creator. Psalm 96:1 says that all the earth "sings to the Lord," and verses 11-12 declare, "Let the heavens be glad, and let the earth rejoice; let the sea roar, and all that fills it; let the field exult, and everything in it! Then shall all the trees of the wood sing for joy before the Lord...."

In Psalm 148, every aspect of Creation is enjoined to give praise to God. Psalm 104 describes the dependence of each part of the Creation on the upholding and sustaining presence of God. It strongly emphasizes God's intimate involvement in the ongoing life of the Creation. The Creation even becomes the place of God's rejoicing (Ps.104:31).

In Psalm 33:6-9, the "word of the Lord" brings forth the Creation. This then becomes a foundation for John's description of Christ as the word through whom all things were made (John 1:3). Likewise, passages also picture God's breath, or Spirit, as upholding all created life (Ps. 104:30).

Noah, Flood, and the Covenant

The Genesis account of God's relationship with Creation and humanity's role, culminates in the story of Noah and the flood in the ninth chapter.

When Noah is born (Gen. 5:29), his name promises relief from the hard labor resulting from God's curse upon the ground. This promise is fulfilled after the flood. The Lord declares, "Never again will I curse the ground because of man.... While the earth remains, seedtime and harvest, cold and heat, summer and winter, day and night, shall not cease" (Gen. 8:21-22).

The account of Noah clarifies the troubling point of "subdue the earth" found in Genesis 1:28, an injunction given to *sinless humanity* before the fall. Different injunctions to till and keep the earth are given in Genesis 2:15. But after the fall and after the flood, when God in effect starts over with Noah and his family, God again repeats the command of Genesis 1:28—"Be fruitful and increase, and fill the earth"—omitting the injunction to "subdue it" (Gen. 9:1). The story of Noah decisively eliminates any notion that God intends for a *fallen humanity* to have oppressive dominion over the earth. For a *sinless humanity*, dominion means stewardship and caring. For a *fallen humanity*, dominion means oppressive rule.

The central point of Noah's story and the ark, however, is the covenant established by God with "living things of every kind." Here for the first time, the word covenant is explicitly used and addressed to humankind. However, God's covenant is established not just with people; it is a covenant with all Creation. The creatures are included explicitly and repeatedly.

Covenant in the Bible is first and foremost an act of mercy. *Berit*, covenant, is formed from the same root as *barah*, meaning to choose, to elect. The covenant is, above all, the act of God's choosing, or electing, a partner. Consequently, the covenant is an act of mercy, of free grace. God makes a covenant with whom God pleases, and when God pleases. Previous to God's offer, God is not bound by anything. When God makes a covenant, God is compelled by nothing but God's own will and God's nature, which is love. The whole covenant bears the mark of this divine act. Although it is a contract, it is God's affair. God determines its limits, its characteristics, its conditions, its signs. The covenant is a binding contract. The terms of this contract are laid down by one party and require mere compliance by the other parties. All God demands of humans is countersigning what God has decided. All the covenants the Bible speaks about are of this type—the covenant with Adam, with Noah, with Abraham and with Moses. In these covenants, God reveals Godself and this self-disclosure is an indication of mercy and election. God reveals Godself not only as the Creator who calls all things into being, but also as one who goes out to meet humans and walk with them as Immanuel. The content of the covenant shows the real character of God.

The covenant is more than just a contract. It establishes a link between God and humans by the exchange of contractual statements. Covenant in the Bible, then, is a solemn promise made by a formal act. The nature of the formal act varies—it could be a spoken or written oath or it may be a symbolic action. But it binds the covenant participants to fulfill the promise made.

The truly striking element in the covenant is the judgment. God judges and manifests God's justice and then God pardons and offers God's covenant. This is true of Adam (Gen. 3). It is also true of Noah (Gen. 9) where God judges the whole earth and condemns it. God sends the flood and brings about justice. Yet God pardons Noah and saves him from destruction. When God has safely brought Noah through judgment, God establishes God's covenant with the whole human race, of which Noah is the representative.

In these examples, the covenant occurs after judgment. The judgment amounts to a death sentence on humans who have separated themselves from God. The notion of grace, of pardon, contained in the covenant offers pardon to the humans sentenced to death. This act of God is not simply an act of goodness. It is the mercy by which God reveals Godself as One whose will is directed toward humans and all of God's Creation.

As the covenant with Adam shows, God always begins the covenant by restoring broken relationship which was the result of humans' action. God does so by proclaiming a will, a will that is not arbitrary but operates in favor of humans and Creation. This is why God chooses to speak of "my covenant." What this seemingly contradictory combination of words mean is that the covenant is really God's.

However, it is not a decree but a contract. God's covenant restores humans as creatures who mirror God, yet they are free creatures or partners with God. God claims as God's own the humans who live by God's grace. God's covenant establishes that humans are capable of making a contract with God; that humans are liberated by God, and that humans live face to face with God. By not imposing conditions, God treats humans as free beings, free to accept or reject God's propositions. The idea of covenant thus includes the idea of human dignity.

God makes two kinds of covenants with people in the Old Testament—conditional and unconditional. The unconditional covenants are the ones in which God makes promises without accompanying obligations. God's covenants with Noah (Gen. 9:8-17), with Abraham (Gen.15), and with David (2 Sam. 7) bind God to the people and to the whole Creation forever, but have no expectation for the people. The Sinai covenant is the most significant example of a conditional covenant in Israel's history (Exod. 19-24).

In the unconditional covenant between God and people, the two parties are unequal. God's contract with humans is in reality a contract of adherence. In this case, God makes adherence a matter of life or death. The covenant will be maintained *if* humans fulfill the conditions set forth by God. Otherwise, the covenant is broken, and the result is pollution. "The earth lies polluted under its inhabitants; for they have transgressed the laws, violated the statutes, broken the everlasting covenant" (Isa. 24:5). As a reminder of humans' creatureliness, humans are tied to the covenant by the threat of death. God gives life and sets down conditions. If humans repudiate the covenant or break it, death results. God destroys those who destroy the Earth (Rev. 11:18).

In this unconditional covenant, humans cannot live as they please. They live under certain physical, moral, or juridical necessities. They cannot live without eating. Nor can they live without reference to the law given in Deuteronomy 6:24—"And the Lord commanded us to do all these statutes...that he might preserve us alive," and in Deuteronomy 16:20—"Justice, and only justice, you shall follow, that you may live." God also gives humans certain rights that are theirs, for example, the right to benefit from the fruitfulness of Creation.

Five times in Genesis 8 and 9, the scope of God's covenant is repeated—a covenant between God and every living creature, with "all living things on earth of every kind." God's faithful love extends to and includes all that has been made. The rainbow is the sign of this promise. The rainbow also reminds us that Creation is central to the drama between God and humanity and that God's promises are directed to the whole Creation—not just to humanity.

All we have said about the covenant so far is real only insofar as Jesus Christ comes to fulfill the covenant, to enact a new and final covenant, giving meaning and value to *all* previous covenants. All these covenants exist only as prophecies and symbols of the covenant in Jesus Christ. Yet Jesus Christ, while fulfilling the covenant, does not modify it. In the new covenant in Jesus Christ, the judgment is pronounced definitively. It is now manifest that humans belong to God, since God ransomed them with the blood of Jesus Christ. In this new covenant the restoration takes place. God shows forth God's righteousness.

The "Wisdom Literature" and Creation

The "wisdom literature" of the Old Testament —Proverbs, Job, Ecclesiastes, and various Psalms—is rich in the theology of Creation. This tradition flows into the New Testament as well.

Through a focus on the Creation, and human experience within it, wisdom literature openly searches for God's truths. The truth that is discovered is then adapted into daily living for a guiding, nurturing presence of God. Thus, wisdom literature consists of observations drawn both from human experience and knowledge of the Creation (e.g., Prov. 3:19-20).

The Wisdom tradition speaks of all of Creation as a living reality which is made by God and returns praise to God, (e.g., Job 7:12; 38:7). In Psalm 114, the sea obeyed God's command to aid the Israelites escaping from the Egyptians. In other passages we read of animals doing God's bidding (e.g., Num. 22:22-35; Jon. 2). One might dismiss such references as mere metaphors, but that seems far too shallow.

At the very least, references to non-human Creation praising and serving God indicate that Creation is not made for humanity, but is also created by and for God. It is given some measure of autonomy as well as interdependence with humans and other Creation. For instance, when God questions Job about Creation, God does not speak of Creation in relation to humanity, but rather praises its power, beauty, strength, and its connection to God. This powerful poetry about Creation is not anthropocentric in its vision of Creation. The creator God of Job relates to the whole cosmos as though it had an integrity of its own, and as though creatures were in some way capable of relation to God.

Within the wisdom literature, the most powerful portrayal of God's relationship to Creation is found in Job, chapters 38 through 42. Job's struggle with disaster is placed in the perspective of God's relationship to all of Creation, of which humanity is only a part. Some of Job's humility comes from his learning that God's concerns and cares are for the entire cosmos, not only for humanity.

Job's approach to nature is one of humility in the knowledge that we humans understand very little about it. Job's attitude is contrary to some presumed attitudes of humanity's dominant role over the Earth. His vision is one of awe and wonder towards the divinely governed ecological balance in the environment—not one of arrogance and self-centeredness.

The Land in Covenant

The land is a gift in covenant. We are participants in Creation. In the people of Israel's experience with the land, we find a model of the promise and peril in humanity's relationship to Creation.

"In the beginning...." Thus begins the cosmic account of Creation contained in the first chapters of Genesis—a history of the origins of the earth and humankind culminating in the Creation of a chosen people. These stories reflect Israel's faith in the one God who is supreme sovereign of the world and whose will is absolute. It is this God who created human beings, creatures who mirror God yet are biologically dependent on nature. Into our hands God has entrusted mastery over God's Creation. This act of Creation was God's first covenant in a series of covenants and revelations to Israel and to us.

The Hebrew Scriptures are a record of the relationship between Israel, the Creation, and Yahweh. Israel's relationship to Creation focuses around land. Hebrew Scripture scholar and theologian Walter Brueggemann goes so far as to say, "Land is a central, if not the central theme of biblical faith."

In biblical teaching, God is the sole owner of the earth. At the heart of the Creation faith is, "The land is mine; for you are strangers and sojourners with me" (Lev. 25:23) and "The earth is the Lord's" (Ps. 24:1). For the Hebrews, the gift of land meant that they had entered into a fruitful relationship with God and with the land itself. No generation had the right to call land its own or do with it what one liked for the land was God's alone. Any kind of monopolizing of land was, therefore, a serious failure in worship. God gave land to Israel as a whole (Deut. 1:8). When land was used by certain families within Israel (Josh. 13 ff.), it was on condition that all members of the tribe or family might share in the fruitfulness of the land. Western Christianity has been extremely weak in proclaiming a gospel of Creation, perhaps because we have deviated far from the conviction of the divine ownership of land, and the equal share of all families in the use of it.

The gift of land is intimately connected to the stability of community. In the Bible, human beings are part of the land, and the community must be preserved. When the basic reverence for land is ignored, it is only too easy for people to be moved about without their consent, for communities to be broken up, for boundaries to be manipulated.

Biblical passages frequently suggest that humanity's rebellion against God results in the land itself suffering, mourning, and becoming unfruitful. If sin gains the upper hand, the curse will be present immediately, and it invariably reacts upon the land. It is defiled, profaned, filled with sin (Lev. 19:29; Num. 35:3; Jer. 2:7; 3:2, 9). All vegetation fades, animals and birds disappear, (Jer. 12:4) the country is no more a habitation of human beings. The moment we begin to use the land selfishly and to reach out to take the fruit which is forbidden by the Lord or destroy Creation's fruitfulness, the ecological balance is upset and nature begins to groan. The land is defiled, and the same land will vomit forth the nation that has become untrue to its moral responsibility (Lev. 18:25,28; 20:22).

In Isaiah 5, we read a condemnation of land-grabbing greed. "Woe to those who join house to house, who add field to field..." (5:8). What's the consequence? "For ten acres of vineyard shall yield but one bath [about six gallons], and a homer [about six bushels] of seed shall yield but an ephah [about one-half bushel]" (5:10). The sin of greed results in the unfruitfulness of the land. The same message is repeated in Isaiah 24:4-6 in sterner terms.

Redeeming the Earth

"How long will the land mourn, and the grass of every field wither?" asks Jeremiah (12:4). The Bible provides the answer in the continual renewal of the created order from the resources of God's grace. The degraded land is restored in "shalom" and, in the words of the Psalm, the face of the earth is renewed (104:30).

The discussion in the section on covenant above is applicable here as well. When the Creation, with all of its life, is reestablished as Noah and all the animals come forth from the ark, God's covenant is announced and repeated over and over again. It's a covenant with "every living creature," a covenant "between me and the earth," says Genesis 9:13. The assurance of the earth's cycles—"seedtime and harvest, cold and heat, summer and winter, day and night" (8:22)—further underscores this promise.

The biblical narrative continually sets forth the saving activity of God's grace, which not only delivers people from oppression but also restores the life of all Creation. Human rebellion has caused a great deal of suffering and violence in God's Creation but it is astonishing that God so loves this Creation that God does not let it perish, but patiently gives it loving care (see John 3:16).

The redemptive promises are set forth in the latter half of Isaiah with images of all the Creation participating in this saving and restoring work of God. God's promise is so compelling that Isaiah describes it as "new heavens and a new earth" (65:17). Redemption opens the world to a new Creation.

Creation Liberated In Christ

Romans 8:19-22 speaks directly about Creation. The New Testament, as a whole, however, provides less direct reference to God's Creation. The Gospels are focused on Jesus' healing and restoring of the broken human condition. Much of the attitude towards all Creation can be gathered from the context of Jesus' own Jewish world and the theology of the Hebrew Bible. In some of the other New Testament material further questions about Creation are raised from the perspective of Jesus' life, death, and resurrection.

In its original biblical context, resurrection expressed an apocalyptic vision of God's vindication of the just. But in the experience of and reflection on Jesus' resurrection, Christians came to understand his resurrection as central to the history of Israel, God's relationship with all humanity, and the restoration of the cosmos. The resurrection became the key not only to the significance and reality of human life, but also of all Creation. All Creation has its relationship to God and its interconnection to one another in the risen Christ. Furthermore, its future and humanity's future, are centered in the risen Christ.

Resurrection in its context came as a shock. For those Jews who believed in resurrection it was an event to occur at the end of time, through which God would vindicate the just and punish the evil. For the Graeco-Roman world, it was an absurdity. But when Jesus appeared on Easter morning, he upset everybody's expectations, compelling his followers to see the world in a radically new way. In particular, the resurrection of his body and promise of future resurrection of others suggests a transformation of the way in which we humans are to relate to the whole physical world to which we belong. This transformation includes a greater value given to the visible Creation in its corporality, and in the hope for human future with the rest of the cosmos.

The New Testament builds on the foundation that integrates Creation into the work of God's redemption. God's role as Creator and sustainer is ascribed to Jesus Christ in the incarnation. With the rainbow covenant (Gen. 9:10) began the long way of salvation for the cosmos. It reached its decisive stage with the reconciliation of the world in the cross of Jesus Christ.

Of Christ, John says, "all things were made through him, and without him was not anything made that was made" (1:3). The hymn of Creation and reconciliation in the Letter to the Colossians says it all: "He (Christ) is the image of the invisible God, the first-born of all Creation; for in him all things were created, in heaven and on earth, visible and invisible.... He is before all things, and in him all things hold together" (Col. 1:15-17).

The rainbow and the cross are not only reminders of God's intention for Creation but also promises of God's faithfulness and reconciliation of Creation. In the cross the world is reconciled to God but it is not yet a new Creation. The final liberation of Creation from all suffering and all violence still remains. Therefore, it is important to pay attention to the biblical images of hope in a new Creation.

Isaiah 11:1-9 portrays the coming Creation where—(1)justice will prevail and be meted out above all to the oppressed and the disadvantaged, and (2) there will be peace between animals and between human beings and animals. Peace is defined as peaceful coexistence between animal and animal, and humans and animals: "They shall not hurt or destroy in all my holy mountain; for the earth shall be full of the knowledge of the Lord as the waters cover the sea" (11:9).

Isaiah 65:17-25 picks up Isaiah 11: "For behold I create new heavens and a new earth; and the former things shall not be remembered.... The wolf and the lamb shall feed together, the lion shall eat straw like the ox.... They shall not hurt or destroy in all my holy mountain says the Lord." This, then leads to chapter 21 of the Revelation to John: "Then I saw a new heaven and a new earth; for the first heaven and the first earth had passed away and the sea was no more: (21:1). In God's new world "God's dwelling is among men" (21:3). Then all tears will be wiped away from their eyes, death will be no more, neither shall there be pain or mourning or crying (21:4). In the design of Creation, death was an obvious condition of life; now that will be otherwise. "And night shall be no more; they need no light of lamp or sun, for the Lord will be their light..." (22:5).

Finally Paul sums up all these pictures of the new Creation in this concise formula: "... Creation itself will be set free from its bondage to decay and obtain the glorious liberty of the children of God" (Rom.8:21). The liberation of Creation, and the glorious freedom of God's children are the ultimate goal for the whole Creation. In faith, we have the strength to trust that God will succeed, and that in spite of the incredible opposition of the powers of darkness and death, God will usher in a new Creation. Because Christ has redeemed us, we can be stewards of Creation.

The following paraphrase of Romans 8:18-25 by Paulos Mar Gregorios might be helpful to us in clarifying the meaning of Creation:

> "For I regard the troubles that befall us in this present time as trivial when compared with the magnificent goodness of God that is to be manifested in us. For the created order awaits, with eager longing, with neck outstretched, the full manifestation of the children of God. The futility or emptiness to which the created order is now subject is not something intrinsic to it. The Creator made the Creation contingent, in his ordering, upon hope; for the Creation itself has something to look forward to—namely, to be freed from its present enslavement to disintegration. The Creation itself is to share in the freedom , in the glorious and undying goodness, of the children of God. For we know how the whole Creation up till now has been groaning together in agony, in a common pain. And not just the nonhuman created order—even we ourselves, as Chris-

tians, who have received the advance gift of the Holy Spirit, are now groaning within ourselves, for we are also waiting—waiting for the transformation of our bodies and for the full experiencing of our adoption as God's children. For it is by that waiting with hope that we are being saved today. We do not hope for something which we already see. Once one sees something, there is no point in continuing to hope to see it. What we hope for is what we have not yet seen; we await its manifestation with patient endurance." (From *Tending the Garden*).

For Reflection and Group Discussion

1. Which points in this chapter were familiar to you from past Bible study experiences? Which were new or surprising?

2. How important to your concern for the earth is "what the Bible says"? What does the Hebraic understanding add to your understanding of the natural world?

3. Few biology texts today teach that all Creation praises God or that the whole earth belongs to God. What kinds of tension do you experience between a modern scientific world view and the biblical perspective on Creation?
   For a more in depth discussion of this question, prepare a handout in advance. Place texts mentioned in this chapter and excerpts from a current science textbook side by side. Read them aloud using two voices.

4. List as many symbols of covenant as you can think of. Include both biblical examples (such as a rainbow) and contemporary examples (such as a wedding ring). Note the title of this book. What does it mean to be in a covenant relationship? How is care for the earth a response to God's covenant?

5. Read Leviticus 18:24-28 and Isaiah 5:8-10; 24:4-6. List contemporary examples of the land mourning or becoming unfruitful due to human sin.

6. What do you think of this author's interpretation of the New Testament? Does Christ's reconciling work extend to all humans or all Creation?
   For a more visual way to contemplate this question, invite a children's class to make a collage illustrating John 3:16.

Have them include outdoor scenes and animals as well as people pictures. Consider planning a worship service centered around the rainbow and the cross.

3
NATURE
AND ITS
RIGHTS

The word nature derives from Latin *nasci,* "to be born," which is fundamental enough, and puts it under the heading of abiding mystery. We do not know the exact meaning of the word or how broad is its meaning. The dictionary definitions include explanations such as "physical power causing the phenomena of the material world," or, "the sum of the surrounding universe."

Nature itself is a mystery. We can know more and more about it, but we can never fully understand it. Job has the best approach to nature: humility in the knowledge that we understand very little about it (Job 38:1-42:6).

The Concept of Nature

Our concept of nature and the ecological crisis we are facing today have a paradoxical relationship. Nature has been and is being transformed by human cultivation, human technology, and human culture. But humanity forms an intrinsic part of this nature, if nature means the sum total of all beings and processes. The paradox refers to the conflict between a view of nature that includes humans (inclusive) and one that marks out a sharp separation between humans and nature (exclusive). Some writers, like Frederick Elder (in his book *Crisis in Eden*) claim that it is the exclusive view that has led to the ecological crisis. In Elder's view, the Christian tradition is strongly exclusive and is therefore responsible for this crisis. He believes that only an inclusive view holds out the possibility for human survival.

The differences in the understanding of the concept of nature makes it problematic. Human culture and history are certainly part of the ongoing process of reality. The question is whether 'nature' is the right term to use to describe the sum total of this reality including humanity, or does the very term amount to a distortion of that reality?

Paulos Mar Gregorios in his book *The Human Presence*, gives four sets of meanings for the word "natural" or "nature." First, in ordinary secular language, "natural" is opposed to contrived or artificial. It is something which happens or comes into being without human intervention. This is nature as the realm of unalterable physical laws, nature as given.

Second, in modern western language, nature has come to have a related second meaning—the non-human part of Creation. Here we include the visible aspects of the Creation around us, namely the elements of earth, air, water, and sky, together with plants and animal life. But we exclude the human-made elements, e.g. cities, buildings, highways, etc.

Third, in Christian theology, nature has two other meanings: i) "Nature" is opposed to "history" and "culture," which are the realm of human action. Protestant theology since the 19th century has tended to emphasize the action of God in history as the central revelation, while usually underplaying God's visible activity in nature. The concept of natural revelation has seemed dangerous, since it may justify the knowledge of God in other religions. And ii) this Protestant distinction between "natural revelation" and "special" or "historical" revelation has its roots in the medieval Roman Catholic distinction, still current, between nature and grace, or between the natural and the supernatural. Grace is God's special and direct action, while nature is given, and has its own laws. Grace can counteract, supplement or overcome nature; it comes from outside or from above nature, and hence is qualified as supernatural.

Fourth, underlying all the above meanings of the word "nature" is another: the given structure or constitution of a person or thing. It is not in the nature of a cat to fly; the hawk and wolf are by nature cruel. Here the reference is both to the given behavior pattern and the expected character of an entity.

The usages noted above reveal important underlying assumptions. They show that the western classical worldview has a hierarchical understanding of Creation. It represents a three-tiered structure with God, whose nature is pure spirit, at the top, and the earth, whose nature is material, at the bottom. So we have a polarity between the spiritual and the material, the divine and the bodily. Ranged in between are the other "orders" of Creation: humans, animals, plants. The closer you get to God, the higher is the moral worth attributed to that order of Creation. Thus, the earth itself is far from God and of little worth.

Nature, in the new three-tiered structure, is at the lowest level as an order with its own given constitution, for both the whole and its parts. Humanity stands on the second level up, creating culture and making history through its actions. On the top level is the realm of the special actions of God, to which terms like revelation, grace, and the supernatural refer. We can call this total structure nature-culture-grace. Under culture, we would include not only history as economic, social, and political action, but also science and technology.

Basing his analysis on Ancient History and the prevalent worldviews, Ronald Manahan, in an essay entitled "Christ as Second Adam" observes that the proper relationship in this three-layered system is *beneficence* to the one beneath and *obedience* to the one above.

Nature in The Bible

The Hebrew tradition is often accused of having desacrilized nature and thereby paved the way for its pillage by humanity. But it is a striking fact that this tradition has no word at all for what we call nature. Biblical scholars tell us that the Greek word for nature, *physis*, occurs only in the later apocryphal books produced outside Palestinian Judaism by Jews living under Greek influence. Not only does the Old Testament have no word for nature (inclusive or exclusive), but it also has no word for what we call the "universe." The closest it comes to this is "heaven and earth."

Neither are there words for "Creation" or for "things."

What that means is that the concept of "nature" is totally alien to the Hebrew tradition as such. The Hebrew had no notion of something "out there" which they were to set about "desacriliz-ing" and then dominating. The command of Yahweh in the book of Genesis was certainly not "to dominate nature," but only to "be fruitful and multiply, and fill the earth and master it, and have rule over the fish of the sea and over the birds of the air and over every living thing that moves on the earth" (Gen.1:28). Mastering the earth and all life on it need not mean mastering "nature" as a whole, which is a much wider concept. This is to say that, in the Old Testament tradition, nature is not an entity to be dominated.

The New Testament, produced under heavy Greek influence, still makes but sparing use of the concept of nature, and only in the classical sense of the God-given nature of an entity. James 3:7 and II Peter 1:4 are clear instances of this. St. Paul also uses the word *physis* with this meaning in Galatians 4:8 in the reference to serving gods who by nature are not gods. Nowhere in the New Testament does the word nature refer to the whole Creation or to its non-human aspect. That, it seems, is a Hellenic legacy in Western Christian thought.

The Rights of Nature

The damage and destruction of nature raises an important question. Could we develop a concept of the rights of future generations and the rights of (extra-human) nature similar to our concept of human rights? "Human rights" arose as an attempt to protect individuals and groups facing concrete historical threats. In the same way, a recognition of threats to nature undergirds the thinking behind assigning rights to nature. The threats to irreplaceable ecosystems and entire species of plants and animals are not hypothetical but very real.

As discussed above, Christian understanding of 'nature' is not uniform. Some Christians consider humans as part of nature and others do not. Some are strongly anthropocentric (human-centered), others are not. Some believe that humans are superior to the rest of the Creation, others deny such human superiority. In light of these diverse beliefs, assigning rights to nature is bound to be controversial. The same will probably apply to the extension of rights to future generations. However, it is important for Christians and for churches to search their souls when it comes to the rights of nature. For example, does the sabbath for the land referred to in Exodus 23 and Leviticus 25-26, imply that land has rights?

At the international level the United Nations has provided a forum for a debate on the issue of the rights of nature by adopting a World Charter for Nature.

World Charter for Nature

A good many Churches have spoken out on the dangers of nuclear annihilation. But few leaders have broadened their vision enough to concede that a constant and increasing rate of destruction of the natural world will have a similar sterilizing effect on the Earth. This issue has not received proper attention from religious leaders. The lack of awareness among the churches with respect to the scriptural prohibitions against the destruction of the Earth (Rev. 11:18) is noteworthy. Somewhat ironically, the first important international document to call attention to the moral dimensions of what is happening is the United Nations' *World Charter for Nature*, approved and solemnly proclaimed by the UN General Assembly in 1982 (see Appendix A). The Charter represents a significant attempt to free nature from its status as a resource permanently and arbitrarily available for use. It attempts an international reconciliation with nature and states that:

(a) Humankind is a part of nature. All life depends on the uninterrupted functioning of natural systems which ensure the supply of energy and nutrients.

(b) Civilization is rooted in nature. Nature has shaped human culture and influenced all artistic and scientific achievement. Living in harmony with nature gives humans the best opportunity for creativity, and for rest and reCreation.

This document then calls for a moral code to guide human interaction with the natural world:

(a) Every form of life is unique, warranting respect regardless of its worth to man, and, to accord other organisms such recognition, man must be *guided by a moral code of action* (italics added).

(b) Man can alter nature and exhaust natural resources by his action or its consequence and, therefore, must fully recognize the urgency of maintaining the stability and quality of nature and of conserving natural resources.

The Charter goes on to propose important general principles. The first two are basic. Number one states: 'That nature shall be respected and its essential processes shall not be impaired.' The second principle deals directly with the threat of extinction: 'The genetic viability of the Earth shall not be compromised; the population levels of all life forms, wild and domesticated, must be, at least, sufficient for their survival, and to this end necessary habitats shall be safeguarded.'

Section 2 specifies what measures need to be taken in order to enhance vital ecosystems and to protect those that are most vulnerable and already seriously damaged.

Section 3 deals with the task of implementing the document. It calls for a knowledge of natural systems and the principles enshrined in the document, challenging nations, local communities and every individual to implement these principles. The document concludes by insisting that:

Each person has a duty to act in accordance with the provisions of the present Charter; acting individually, in association with others or through participating in the political process, each person shall strive to ensure that the objectives and requirements of the present Charter are met.

This is a prophetic document. It calls for extensive changes in the lifestyle of individuals and whole societies in order to conserve nature's capacity to regenerate. We are thus challenged to be aware of the long-term consequences of our everyday behavior. We are called to consume less.

Unfortunately, in spite of its comprehensive approach, the *World Charter of Nature* has not received much attention in the media. Churches could take up its challenge, bring it to members' attention and encourage programs to implement its recommendations.

The End of Nature

Bill McKibben's book, *The End of Nature,* has received a great deal of attention since publication in 1989. A powerful, disturbing book, it has been highly praised and roundly criticized in nearly equal proportions. McKibben's thesis is that humankind's imprint on the world has become so pervasive that the idea of nature as an independent, limiting force is all but lost to us. We now have the power to manipulate the material of nature inside (biotechnology) and out (planetary resource management). But our dominance may be working against us. Spiritually, we are losing contact with the "other" in our lives; materially we are putting ourselves at the mercy of consequences we cannot foresee.

In addition to discussing global warming and other ecological ills, McKibben deals with the question of how we might adapt to a world we have so relentlessly made over in our own image. Planet Earth's survival is our most important topic for discussion and McKibben's viewpoint cannot be ignored in such discussion.

For Reflection and Group Discussion

1. What comes to mind when you hear the word "nature?" What difference does including humans as part of nature make in your attitude toward it?

2. Reread paragraph four i) (p. 32) on God's activity in nature/God's activity in history. How do you see God at work in nature? Is this an important part of your faith? If not, how do you respond to those who stress natural revelation? If so, what does nature reveal about God? For an interesting perspective on this latter question, see Annie Dillard, *Pilgrim at Tinker Creek*, chps. 8-9.

3. How do you understand Genesis 1:26-31? How would you describe the biblical view of nature?

4. Scan the World Charter for Nature in Appendix A. Work together to write a covenant with nature appropriate to your local area. Be as specific as you can.

5. Read the address attributed to Chief Seattle in Appendix H.1. Compare his understanding of nature with those found in Genesis or the World Charter for Nature. For a more focused discussion, prepare a handout in advance with excerpts from these three texts side by side.

PART II

Planet Earth

4
THE EARTH:
OUR HOME

Creation comprises the whole universe, known and unknown throughout the boundaries of space and time,
from the beginning until now and into the future. Much of the
universe is beyond our knowledge and imagination. We will,
therefore, focus our attention on the tiny fragment of it where
we live—the Earth.

History

Earth is a minute fragment of a universe that is believed by
many astronomers to have come into existence as the result of a
cataclysmic explosion of a single mass of highly concentrated
matter some ten billion years ago. Out of this explosion evolved
the galaxies, such as our Milky Way, that are made up of many
billions of stars that are known to exist in the heavens.

Where earth had its origin and how it came to be have been
subjects of much speculation among mathematicians and
astronomers, geologists and biologists, physicists and chemists,
and philosophers and theologians. Some of the more modern
concepts of highly capable scientists especially concerned with
this subject appear sufficiently conclusive to make the history of
the Earth widely accepted.

Earth, located some 93 million miles out in space from Sun
and revolving around it once every 365 days at the speed of
about twenty-two miles a second, is believed to have come into
existence largely as a gaseous mass that began to solidify to its
present form some 4.5 billion years ago. The Sun and other

planets of the solar system are thought to have been formed at about the same time.

Earth is changing and it has always changed. A sedimentary record spanning much of Earth's 4.5-billion-year history attests to continual change throughout past ages. Species have come and gone: many more have gone than have remained behind. Climates have shifted, mountains have risen and eroded away, continents have split and moved thousands of miles to open new seas. On this time scale the history of humans is vanishingly small.

Modern humans appear to have arisen 2 million or so years ago during the second of two ice ages that have occurred in the half-billion years since the beginning of the fossil record. The first ice age occurred 250-300 million years ago and lasted 20-30 million years. The most recent Ice Age started about 5 million years ago in the Southern Hemisphere and about 2.5 million years ago in the north. A retreat of the Ice Age that began only 8 to 16 thousand years ago has left the world we know. The cause of the fluctuations in climate that produce ice ages is unknown. The changes in climate, however, have obviously been profound, some of them within the span of humanity's short time on earth.

It may be useful for us to orient ourselves in time and space. For all earthly purposes, time began approximately 4.5 billion years ago when the planet was formed. After that, it took approximately 1.5 billion years for the first organized forms of living things to emerge from tidal pools and around 2.9 billion years more, for human's remotest known ancestors to appear. Roughly 2 million years later, the first human-like creatures developed, and 1.96 million years after that, the first members of our species established themselves.

It took 30,000 years or so for Stone Age agriculture to begin: an invention that "overnight" permitted humanity's numbers eventually to exceed the 10 million that the planet supported without farming and animal husbandry. Nearly 5,000 more years elapsed before humans established their first agricultural civilization. All this while, one could say that humanity (and all its ancestors) had lived *within* nature; the "organic" forms of their art, tools, habitations, etc., reflected this relationship. Then roughly 2,400 years later, the so-called "Sixth Century Revolution" in religion and philosophy swept through China, India, Persia, Greece and the Middle East, and as symbolized by depictions at the time of Adam's expulsion from the Garden of Eden, humans found themselves *outside* of nature. Human arts, crafts and structures reflected this change in the human-nature relationship in their formal, sober, religious aspects. Human beings experienced their first loss of innocence.

In the latter half of the 18th century, some 2,300 years or so later, the Industrial Revolution endowed humans with new powers *over* nature, changing the relationship once again. The mood of humans' works changed with it. Systematized, mechanized, technically intricate designs and patterns began to dominate.

One hundred years of spreading industrialization (largely in the Western world), prepared the human mind for the next major shift. Philosophers of the stature of Locke, Bacon, Mill, Comte, and Hume fostered the self-confident themes which for the first time suggested the possibility of human's ultimate conquest over their natural domain. So for at least the past 130 years, humans have been, in effect, pitted *against* nature. More recent developments in the arts and other enterprises include virtual deification of technology, the computer seen as an analogue to human brain, a depersonalization of industry. These suggest to some that humans have, in fact, pitted themselves against their *own* nature.

It should be noted, too, that human beings lost their innocence twice in the past century: once when they developed the capability and philosophical attitude to assault nature in what turned out to be criminal ways, (we frequently hear the phrase "rape of the earth," these days), and now very recently, when they became aware of their crimes. Thus, in no way can humans again be thought to be innocent with regard to their relationship to their environment.

The fact that Planet Earth is finite and has a limited carrying capacity is now unavoidable. The concept of carrying capacity is used in the management of animal population where the carrying capacity of a territory (for a given species of animals) is defined as that number that can be supported indefinitely without degradation of the territory. If this capacity is transgressed, by even a small amount, carrying capacity in subsequent years is diminished. If transgression occurs every year, the carrying capacity enters a downward spiral from which there may be no recovery, ever.

The human environment can be considered in terms of area, volume, matter and energy within the earth-sun system. Spaceship Earth, as the planet has come to be called, is limited in area and volume that is humanly occupiable, in kind and quality of consumable resources and in its capacity to recover from physical abuse (e.g., atmospheric pollution) and continue to support life.

The other prime factor in earth's "carrying capacity," is solar energy. Sunlight is the only biologically consumable input to our spaceship. Cosmic rays have biological effects in the production of mutations but do not add significantly to the biosphere's energy budget. A fixed amount of solar energy falls upon the Earth in a given amount of time, and only a small percentage of that energy is convertible by photosynthesis into living substance.

Together, these factors—living space, raw materials, solar energy and the earth's environmental resilience—determine the planet's capacity for supporting life. But what are the actual limits to this equation and how immutable are they? This is a more difficult question than it might seem, for what may be a limiting factor under one set of circumstances may not be under another. Enterprising humans have stretched Earth's limitations many times in the past and no doubt will try to do so in the future.

For example, humans expanded the living space that was initially accessible to them through the application of fire and other forms of energy, with tools and the use of raw materials for acquiring food, clothing and shelter. By developing better and better means of transportation and communication, humans extended their range of movement and flexibility in selecting living spaces that they could not otherwise inhabit. They also augmented the carrying capacity of the space they occupied with the development of agriculture and by the redefinition of "nature" as "natural resource." To many, this redefinition has been made complete so that *all* of nature is now considered a resource. The discovery and exploitation of raw materials and the Creation of technologies by which to use energy and materials have made it possible to support their growing numbers.

Yet, there are limits in a finite world. The earth is finite and exponential growth cannot continue without soon exceeding all physical bounds. We humans need to remember that we live in two worlds—the ecosphere or the natural world that all living things require, and the technosphere which is the world of our own Creation: farms, homes, cars, food, clothing, the arts and so on.

It seems our two worlds are at war.

Ecology

The natural world is complex and beautiful. The Creation is a silent partner in our lives and in the composite of forces and processes that are usually taken for granted, but without which we could not survive.

The Age of Ecology began July 16, 1945, with a dazzling fireball of light and a swelling mushroom cloud of radio-active gases above the desert outside Alamogordo, New Mexico. For the first time in some two million years of human history, there existed a force capable of destroying the entire fabric of life on the planet. One kind of fallout from the atomic bomb was the beginnings of widespread, popular ecological concern around the globe. It began, appropriately, in the United States, where the nuclear era was launched. The devastation of Bikini atoll, the poisoning of the atmosphere with strontium-90, and the threat of irreversible genetic damage struck public conscious-ness with an impact that dust storms and predator deaths could never have had. Here was a question of the survival of living things, humans included, everywhere in the world.

Ecology is the area of human understanding that deals with the interrelatedness of living things and the non-living environment. It is more specifically defined as that branch of science that deals with the structure and function of nature. Since the term "ecology" is derived from the Greek *oikos* (meaning household or home), ecology may also be simply defined as a study of organisms 'at home,' with everything that affects them there. In its broadest sense, it is the science of planetary housekeeping. For the environment is, so to speak, the house created on the earth *by* living things *for* living things. Included in this 'at home' is the study of living beings, the place in which they live, and the interaction among and between the living and non-living components of the place being studied. So ecology attempts to understand the complex web of interactions and interdepen-dencies in a particular environment or ecosystem. The ecosys-tem being studied might be a meadow, a freshwater lake, a mangrove swamp, an island, a continent, an ocean or finally the Earth itself.

Ecology reminds us that human beings are part of the 'house.' Humans have evolved interdependently with the Earth and its creatures over a few million years and we deceive ourselves if we ever think we can survive without the Earth. If, however, we continue to ignore the Earth as we are doing now, we may bring the whole house down around us.

As an emerging discipline, ecology combines insights from numerous sciences: biology, genetics, biochemistry, zoology, chemistry, geology and geography. Its particular focus is not on the properties of a single organism, but on the interrelatedness between living forms and their environment. The hallmark of the study is its relational, dynamic perspective.

In the last two to three decades, the term ecology has become popular in the US. Today, ecology is one of the most active fields of scientific research, and our knowledge about the environment has trebled in the last two decades. Much effort has been given to correct the consequences resulting from decades of environmental neglect which threaten the integrity of Creation—littering, pollution, land degradation and so on. However, not enough attention has been paid to bringing home to all that environmental processes are universal in occurrence and that our survival and well-being are dependent upon the proper functioning of those principles.

One of the most important concepts of ecology is that everything in the Creation is related to everything else. *Interrelatedness*, however important it may be, is hard to conceptualize. It is very difficult, for example, to see the functional and ecological ties between the burning of rain forests in Brazil and the survival of algae in a lake somewhere. Ecologists often use the expression "web of life" as a means to describe the important functional links in the environment. Everyone should be aware of the concept of interrelatedness.

Homo sapiens is by far the dominant species in the environment today. Human intellect and technological skills are capable of altering radically any portion of the environment. Historically, most of human activities have been environmentally destructive. Either we do not care what happens to our environment, or we have not understood the basic lesson of the interrelatedness of nature.

Several of the chapters in this book provide details of many of our environmental problems. It is important to keep in mind that every ecological principle applies to people as much as it does to any other living creature. Remember always, that we are both *in* and *of* the environment—not somehow apart from it.

Ecosystems

An ecosystem, or ecological system, functions as an interacting whole in nature. It is an open-energy system in which solar energy is incorporated into organic compounds by green plants. Energy is transferred within the plant, from plant to animal, from animal to animal, and finally through decomposing organisms, such as fungi and bacteria. In this process, the original potential energy in plants is degraded from concentrated form to greater and greater dispersion until all of it is dissipated as heat.

An ecosystem is somewhat like an open reservoir, with energy in place of water flowing through the system. Maintaining the ecosystem requires a constant input of energy, which moves through the system and eventually is lost to the system. Through feedback mechanisms, the system maintains a certain degree of stability in what is known as steady state, or homeostasis. A single cell and its microenvironment, whether free-living or part of a tissue system, may be an ecosystem. More common examples are a forest, a stream, a lake, a marsh, estuary or ocean. The entire ecosphere, the envelope of all living things and their sustaining environment, is an ecosystem. Ecosystems are real, dynamic entities. They are basic units of ecological study, of interrelatedness.

Energy is a necessary input. The sun is the ultimate source for the biosphere, and directly supports most natural ecosystems within the biosphere. But there are other energy sources that may be important for many ecosystems, for example, wind, rain, water flow, or fuel (the major source for the modern city). It is through the transfer of energy that ecosystems are also ordered. As a stream flows downhill with eventual loss of its energy, a turbine and dam can use a portion of this energy to build up something else.

Ecosystems are never completely static; they are dynamic realities. Nevertheless most ecosystems in their natural environment develop a dynamic stability unless significant changes are introduced from the outside to disrupt the pattern of relationships. In some situations, outside influences are so massive that an ecosystem collapses. For example, high concentrations of nitrogen and phosphorous entering a body of fresh water can induce a proliferation of algae which suffocate many of the traditional life-forms in the lake and leave the lake itself biologically 'dead.' When the focus of the study widens from single ecosystems to the Earth itself, many ecologists fear that changes presently taking place are so massive that they will cause the collapse of essential ecosystems like the oceans. The consequences would be disastrous for all life forms, including human beings.

In every ecosystem, there are two basic kinds of interdependent components that interact with each other in ranges from obligatory to casual. On the one hand are the non-living, inanimate, or *abiotic* components. This includes the soil (partly living), water, chemicals, atmosphere and gases, sunlight, temperature, and many physical processes such as currents, pressures, and gradients. Everything in an ecosystem that is not alive is a part of the abiota.

The *biotic* component consists of the many and diverse living organisms. A forest as an ecosystem, for example, has such varied living things as trees, shrubs, birds, insects, earthworms, and mammals. Amid this enormous diversity, we would find three different types of biota, based on their functional roles in the ecosystem. Only a rare ecosystem does not contain all three types of biota. The three types are—the producers, the consumers and the decomposers.

Producers: These are the green plants or trees in a forest or microscopic algae in a lake or ocean, that capture the sun's energy and convert it into carbohydrate materials like sugars. They are also called *autotrophs* or self feeders. This overall process is called *photosynthesis.* Photosynthesis is involved in the production of food energy by plants using raw materials from the abiotic environment.

The photosynthetic equation is: carbon dioxide + water with the help of solar energy, enzymes and chlorophyll, produce carbohydrates + oxygen.

Photosynthesis is one of the most important biological processes for it alone accounts for almost the entire conversion of abiotic energy into chemical food-energy molecules.

Consumers: These are the animals, ranging from microscopic creatures in aquatic ecosystems to huge elephants and whales.

They are called consumers because they use or consume chemical compounds initially produced by the producers. They are
totally dependent upon the producers for they lack the ability
to convert abiotic energy into chemical energy. They live by
eating plants (herbivores), or by eating animals that, in turn, ate
plants (carnivores). Thus animals are appropriately called consumers or *heterotrophs* (nourished from others). There is a
definite, one-way transfer of food energy from producers to
herbivores to carnivores, thus producing a food chain.

Decomposers: These are the organisms of decay and are
represented principally by bacteria and fungi. Decomposers are
present everywhere in ecosystems and are particularly common, for example, at the bottom of a lake or on the forest floor.
Their role in the ecosystem is to effect decay—to break down
dead organisms (leaves, stems, bones, flesh) and thereby convert
their constituent molecules back into the atoms of which they
are built. As heterotrophs, decomposers feed on the decaying
bodies of other organisms.

Although decomposers are small and often inconspicuous,
they are, nonetheless, both extraordinarily numerous and important to an ecosystem. They reduce the vast bulks of organis-
mic remains to their elemental particles which then are again
available to be used by other organisms.

Every typical ecosystem contains producers, consumers,
decomposers, and many abiotic factors. Each organism is totally
and utterly dependent—directly or indirectly—upon sunlight
for light, warmth, and above all energy for life processes. The
various facets of an ecosystem are all interrelated. And all
ecosystems on our planet are tied together in marvelously
beautiful and intricate patterns of interdependence. Ecologists
often refer to the spherical envelope around the earth in which
all of the ecosystems are located and tied together functionally,
as the *ecosphere* (or *biosphere*).

The Biosphere

The source of all life is the earth's thin skin of air, water, and
soil, and the radiant solar fire that bathes it. Here, several billion
years ago, life was created and was nourished by the Earth's
substance. As it grew, life unfolded its old forms transforming
the earth's skin and new ones adapting to these changes. Living
things multiplied in number, variety, and habitat until they
formed a global network, becoming deftly enmeshed in the

surroundings they had themselves created. This is the *biosphere,* the home that life has built for itself on the planet's outer surface.

Any living thing that hopes to live on the earth must fit into the biosphere or perish. The environmental crisis is a sign that the finely sculptured fit between life and its surroundings has begun to erode. Why, after millions of years of harmonious co-existence, have the relationships between living things and their earthly surroundings begun to collapse? Where did the fabric of the ecosphere begin to unravel? How far will the process go? How can we stop it and restore the broken links?

Understanding the biosphere is hard because, to the modern mind, it is a curiously foreign place. We have become accustomed to think of separate, singular events, each dependent upon a unique, singular cause. But in the biosphere every effect is also a cause. An animal's waste becomes food for soil bacteria; what bacteria excrete nourishes plants; animals eat the plants. Such ecological cycles are hard to fit into human experience in the age of technology, where machine A always yields product B, and product B, once used, is cast away, having no further meaning.

The first great fault of humans in the biosphere is that we have broken out of the circle of life, converting its endless cycles into human-made, linear events. Oil is taken from the ground, distilled into fuel, burned in an engine, converted thereby into noxious fumes, which are emitted into the air. At the end of the line is smog. Other human-made breaks in the biosphere's cycles spew out toxic chemicals, sewage, heaps of rubbish—testimony to our power to tear the ecological fabric that has, for millions of years, sustained the planet's life.

Suddenly we have discovered what we should have known long before: that the biosphere sustains people and everything they do; that anything that fails to fit into the biosphere is a threat to its finely balanced cycles; that wastes are not only unpleasant, not only toxic, but more meaningfully, evidence that the biosphere is being driven towards collapse.

Carl Linnaeus, the renowned Swedish student of the 18th century, to whom we owe our present-day system of plant and animal classification, in a 1791 essay entitled *The Oeconomy of Nature,* writes:

> "*By the Oeconomy of Nature we understand the all-wise disposition of the Creator in relation to natural things, by which they are fitted to produce general ends,*

and reciprocal uses. All things contained in the compass of the universe declare, as it were, with one accord the infinite wisdom of the Creator. For whatever strikes our senses, whatever is the object of our thoughts, are so contrived, that they concur to manifest the divine glory, i.e., the ultimate end which God proposed in all his works. Whoever duly turns his attention to the things on this our terraqueous globe, must necessarily confess, that they are so connected, so chained together, that they all aim at the same end and to this end a vast number of intermediate ends are subservient...."

... "It is sufficient for us, that nothing is made by Providence in vain, and that whatever is made, is made with supreme wisdom. For it does not become us to pry too boldly into all the designs of God. Let us not imagine, when these rapacious animals sometimes do us mischief, that the Creator planned the order of nature according to our private principles of oeconomy...."

... "We, of the human race, who were created to praise and adore our Creator, unless we choose to be mere idle spectators, should and in duty ought to be affected with nothing so much as the pious consideration of this glorious palace (of Creation). Most certainly if we were to improve and polish our minds by the knowledge of these things; we should, besides the great use which would accrue to our oeconomy, discover the more excellent oeconomy of nature, and more strongly admire it when discovered."

At this moment in history ecology has much to teach each of us as individuals and as a human family so that we may begin to care more for the only home we all share—planet Earth, a home gifted to us by a Creator who does all things well. For the life-sustaining beauty of the created Earth declares the glory of God, as God declares its goodness. Thus the more we understand of the intricacy of a healthy ecosystem, the more we learn of the Creator. Nevertheless, that intricacy reminds us of our creatureliness: for, despite the fact that starvation does not generally occur within ecosystems, the balance is maintained by death. And death—of a plant, an animal, or of another person— reminds us that we too are creatures. We are a part of the biosphere.

God has created us as God has all other creatures. We, too, are organisms living within a rich but limited world. We share with all creatures fundamental biological needs: the need for energy and minerals, for food, for air, for water. We can now get so far away from the earth that we can see earth and moon as two small spheres against blackness; nevertheless, we are bound to earth, still enmeshed in its cycles of life. The life of the Earth is *our* life, and we depend upon it. Thus the Christian respect for Creation has a twofold source: believers delight in it as God's work and respect it as they respect their own bodies—for in a sense the biosphere is our extended body.

For Reflection and Group Discussion

1. Plan a guided meditation for your group covering the entire sweep of earth's history. Place yourself on a cliff overlooking a familiar valley. Imagine this valley under-water as it might once have been; then under ice. Imagine a prehistoric scene; then move to the human era. What kinds of Native American dwellings might once have stood there: How might his valley have looked when it was home to the first European settlers: How might it have looked 50 years ago? Close your meditation with Ps. 103:15-18 (we are as grass but God's love endures.)
   How does this long view of a familiar place affect your outlook on life?

2. This book affirms that God is Creator of all. It also assumes that life evolved over a long period of time. Does your group find these two assumptions compatible? Why or why not?

3. This chapter notes a progression in the human/nature relationship from *within* nature to *outside* to *over* and finally *against* nature. Do you agree with this description of human history? Describe times you have experienced yourself to be within, over or against nature.

4. Ecology stresses the connectedness of all things and the intricacy of these relationships. Spend a bit of time in either background reading or backyard observation. Find at least one example of this interrelatedness you had not seen before to share with your group.

PART III

Human
Degradation
Of Creation

5

GLOBAL
WARMING

The Greenhouse Effect

The "Greenhouse effect" is a phrase popularly used to describe the increased warming of the earth's surface and lower atmosphere due to increased levels of carbon dioxide and other atmospheric gases. Like the glass panels of a greenhouse, these gases let heat in but prevent some of it from going back out. If it weren't for the greenhouse effect, temperatures at the earth's surface today would be some 33°C (60°F) colder than they are, and life as we know it could not exist. Scientists are now debating whether the amount of these "greenhouse gases" will soon be increased by human actions to levels harmful to life on earth. A rate of climate change tens of times faster than the average rate of natural change is feared by the middle of the next century. How much and how fast temperatures will change and how these changes will alter accustomed patterns of rainfall, drought, growing seasons, sea level, and so on is controversial. But the greenhouse effect as a scientific proposition is as widely accepted a theory as there is in the earth sciences today. The greenhouse phenomenon is an essential feature of the earth's atmosphere, providing a warm temperature band conducive to the emergence of life on the planet. The natural greenhouse cover has varied little over eons of history.

Human activities since the Industrial Revolution have dramatically altered the composition of the global atmosphere. A number of gases, emitted in small but significant amounts, absorb infrared radiation reflected from the surface of the earth. As the concentrations of these heat-absorbing gases increase, average global temperatures will rise.

Emissions of carbon dioxide (CO_2) are the single largest cause of elevated terrestrial temperatures from the greenhouse effect. They account for approximately one-half of the problem. Concentrations of CO_2 in the range of 280 parts per million (ppm), together with water vapor in the atmosphere, established the preindustrial equilibrium temperature of the planet. Since the middle of the 19th century atmospheric CO_2 levels have increased by about 25 percent to approximately 350 ppm. They continue to rise by approximately 0.4 percent per year. Elevated CO_2 concentrations result primarily from the intensified burning of fossil fuels—coal, oil, and natural gas—which liberates the chemical in varying amounts. Coal burning releases the most CO_2, while the combustion of quantities of natural gas and oil needed to produce the same amount of energy results in only about 57 percent and 83 percent as much CO_2, respectively. Almost half the rise in atmospheric CO_2 since the beginning of the industrial era has occurred in the last 30 years.

The world's forests are vast storehouses or "sinks" of carbon. Worldwide loss of forest cover, by releasing this vast stockpile of carbon into the atmosphere as CO_2, aggravates the greenhouse problem. Deforestation in Third World countries is particularly severe, with the destruction of tropical forests in developing countries like Brazil and Indonesia exceeding 27 million acres annually from activities such as burning, logging, and conversion to agricultural and pastureland. Indeed, the release of CO_2 into the atmosphere as a result of deforestation amounts to 2-10 billion tons annually.

Concentrations of a second important greenhouse gas, nitrous oxide (N_2O), have also been rising, probably because of heavier fossil fuel use, greater agricultural activity, and other ecological disturbances. Average global atmospheric levels of N_2O at the end of 1985 were approximately 300 parts per billion (ppb) and are increasing at an annual rate of 2 percent. Both CO_2 and N_2O, unlike some conventional pollutants, are very stable compounds. CO_2 remains in the upper atmosphere for decades after its release and N_2O for considerably more than a century. Consequently, without major reductions in emissions of these gases with long atmospheric lifetimes, their concentrations will continue to grow.

A group of volatile chemicals known as chloroflurocarbons (CFCs) is believed to be currently responsible for 15-20 percent of the global warming trend. These chemicals, unlike CO_2 are strictly synthetic and are not known in nature. They are described in the section on ozone depletion.

Methane, the principal component of natural gas, is another significant climate-modifying chemical. It has an atmospheric residence of about 11 years. Average global concentrations of methane were approximately 1,700 ppb at the end of 1985 and are increasing by about 1 percent per year, the highest rate of any naturally occurring greenhouse gas, for reasons that are not now clear. Animal husbandry and rice cultivation have been identified as major sources of increased methane emissions. Coal mining and landfills are also significant sources, likely to grow in the future.

Low-level ozone is another greenhouse gas. Although ozone in the stratosphere is beneficial, this highly unstable chemical is the leading component of photochemical smog pollution at the earth's surface.

While greenhouse gases disperse relatively quickly throughout the global atmosphere after release, industrial emissions of these heat-absorbing chemicals are highly concentrated in the developed world. In 1985, 23 percent of total global CO_2 emissions of more than 20.5 billion tons of CO_2 originated in the United States—the single largest emitting country and the highest per capita contributor among industrial countries to the greenhouse problem. The second biggest contribution came from the Soviet Union, with 19 percent of total CO_2 emissions. Western Europe emitted 15 percent of the total, Japan 5 percent, and the People's Republic of China 11 percent. Other developing countries together accounted for only 20 percent of total industrial CO_2 emissions.

Emissions of CFCs are even more strongly skewed. In 1980, the United States produced roughly 28 percent of the global total of approximately 817,300 tons of CFCs. Western Europe produced about 30 percent, industrialized Asian countries 12 percent, and the East-bloc countries an estimated 14 percent. The entire developing world accounted for just slightly more than 2 percent of this amount.

Carbon dioxide makes up only a thirtieth of 1 percent of the atmosphere, but together with water vapor and other trace gases such as methane and the chloroflurocarbons (CFCs) that have also been pouring into the atmosphere it plays a major role in determining the earth's climate. The trace gases intensify the CO_2-induced greenhouse effect by between 50 and 150 percent.

Human beings have produced the CFCs, and human beings are at least partly responsible, if indirectly, for the methane increase, even though the gas is generated by a variety of natural processes. Bacteria produce methane when they break down organic matter in such locales as rice paddies and the guts of cows and termites. Still, it can be argued that people, by killing trees, have made more dead wood for termites to feed on. Certainly they have raised more cows and rice to nourish the rapidly growing human population.

Consequences of Greenhouse Warming

The international scientific community now agrees that the build-up in the atmosphere of CO_2 and other gases from automobiles and factories could have sweeping and far-reaching effects on the earth's climate. By the middle of the next century, average global temperatures may have risen by as much as 3°-9° F. A temperature change, as large and rapid as this would exceed any previously experienced in human history. It would alter weather patterns, disrupt food production and raise sea levels.

The most commonly discussed effect of rising temperatures is the partial melting of the polar ice caps. This would create a rise in the global sea level of one meter or more (several fold more, in some estimates). Billions of dollars worth of coastland, it is estimated, would be submerged. Storms would flood settlements on flat coastal plains. Both people and wildlife would be driven inland. The salty oceans would surge upstream through the mouths of rivers. The warming would intensify the evaporation of water basins, reservoirs, and rivers, reducing fresh-water supplies everywhere. Relatively drier regions—for example, the western United States—would be particularly hard hit.

An increase of 5-7 feet in sea level would submerge 30-80 percent of America's coastal wetlands, which are crucial to commercially important fisheries. Existing coastal development may prevent new wetlands from forming.

The increase in elevation of the oceans will also seriously affect the approximately 50 percent of the earth's population that inhabits coastal regions. Entire countries, such as the Maldives, could disappear. A rise in sea level of only 3 feet could flood an area of the Nile Delta that constitutes 12-15 percent of Egypt's arable land, produces a similar proportion of the Egyptian annual gross national product (GNP), and is home to a comparable percentage of the country's 51.4 million people. In Bangladesh, a 3 foot rise would inundate 11.5 percent of the country's land area, displace 9 percent of the 112.3 million people in this densely populated country, and threaten 8 percent of the annual GNP.

A warmer climate, with lower rainfall, would turn arable croplands into dry grasslands or even into desert. Regions of agricultural productivity could shift at the expense of the American Midwest, which currently has some of the most fertile soils in the world. A warming of only 3.6° F could decrease wheat and cereal yields by 3-17 percent. Computer models predict continental drying in middle latitudes, which means that parched soils, scorching droughts, and massive heat waves, like those that devastated crops in the Midwest in summer 1988, could become commonplace. Water levels in the Great Lakes could drop by a foot, interfering with navigation for ocean-going vessels. Forests, many of them economically productive, could begin to die off as early as year 2000 if they prove unable to adjust to rapidly shifting climatic zones. Animals would try to migrate to more suitable ecological niches, but they would be blocked by highways and fences. In the summer, people would swelter in cities five to seven degrees warmer—and warmer for more days—than they are now.

A working group of the United Nations Intergovernmental Panel on climate change strongly affirmed global warming theories. The group's May 1990 report said that if nothing at all was done, the global mean temperature could rise 5.4° F by the end of the 21st century, leading to some of the consequences described above.

The report also said that just to stabilize atmospheric concentrations of carbon dioxide, nitrous oxide and CFCs at today's levels, their output would have to be cut more than 60 percent immediately. Depending on how much was actually done to cut emissions, it said, global mean temperature would still keep rising between 0.1°C (0.18°F) and 0.2°C (0.36°F) per decade. According to the UN report, global mean surface air temperature has already increased by 0.3°C (0.54°F) to 0.6°C(1.08°F) over the last 100 years, with the five average warmest years all occurring in the 1980s.

So far, there has been only one major step to control greenhouse gases. In 1989, major industrialized countries pledged to ban production of CFCs, used as refrigerants and propellants, by the end of this century. The developing countries are being asked to agree to a similar ban.

Ozone Depletion

Scientists have grown increasingly worried about the health of the Earth's ozone shield, a fragile canopy of stratospheric gas 13 to 35 miles above the surface that blocks harmful radiation from the sun. Life on earth depends as much on this shield as it does on the presence of oxygen and water.

Among the disturbing changes in the reality around us is the depletion of the ozone gas that normally forms this protective layer. Ozone is a molecule of oxygen made up of three oxygen atoms. Its depletion was first recognized in 1984 when a British survey team discovered a gaping hole in the ozone layer over Antarctica. The catalyst of the depletion was the release into the atmosphere of chloroflurocarbons (CFCs), a family of human-made chemical compounds that make spray cans spray and air conditioners cool.

CFCs are stable gases used industrially as propellants, for refrigeration and air conditioners, as well as for making foam cushions, foams for packaging and insulation and solvents. It is estimated that 80 percent of the CFCs manufactured over the past thirty years have yet to reach the stratosphere, and production continues.

Ozone molecules are much less abundant than the type of oxygen essential for the breathing of living organisms, but they play an important part in the biosystem: they prevent much of the sun's ultraviolet radiation, which can be highly injurious to life, from penetrating to the Earth's surface.

A team of six scientists-adventurers who returned in March 1990 from a seven month International Trans-Antarctica expedition recently faced a deadly hazard their predecessors never did: they spent two months in sunlight that was streaming through the gigantic hole in the Earth's protective ozone layer. The men were exposed to what scientists fear may be in store for all human life if ozone depletion is allowed to continue. The expedition's leader, Will Steger, said, "It was like standing under an ultraviolet sun lamp for 24 hours a day. We had to cover our bodies totally. One member of our team forgot and exposed his skin for a few hours. He suffered severe burns. His face swelled. He was nauseated for days." Special fabrics resistant to ultraviolet radiation were used in the group's clothing. Ordinary clothing would just fall apart.

The expedition was taken for monitoring damage to the ozone layer and to focus human-made threats to the environment. Human-made pollutants that break down in sunlight and release ozone-eating chlorine are estimated to have destroyed as much as 2 percent of the ozone layer, with the greatest detectable damage over Antarctica each September and October. Unique weather conditions over Antarctica form a whirlpool, or vortex, of frigid air that traps the CFCs in the atmosphere. These pollutants then chemically combine with the ozone umbrella to break it down molecule by molecule.

Although the ozone hole seals up in warm weather, it is getting bigger and lasting longer. Moreover, recent scientific surveys indicated the beginnings of a similar hole over the Arctic, which if it moved south could affect heavily populated areas.

The Environmental Protection Agency, in fact, has estimated that unless ozone depletion is stopped by strict antipollution measures, each 1 percent loss in protection may ultimately result in 3 percent to 6 percent more cases of skin cancer—about 60 million additional cases in the US alone.

The effects of the ozone hole already are being felt. Each spring in the Southern Hemisphere, as Texas-sized patches of ozone-depleted Antarctic air drift northward over Australia and New Zealand, researchers have measured temporary increases in ultraviolet radiation as high as 20 percent.

Australian residents have the highest rate of skin cancer in the world due to their light complexion and heavy exposure to sunlight. But because of the increased risk from the ozone hole-associated radiation, TV stations there now report daily ultraviolet readings and issue warnings for people to stay inside during the worst spells.

Antarctica with its fragile ecology, also is under intense study because of possible extinction of plankton, single-celled plants that serve as the beginning of the food chain for the rich marine life that abounds in Antarctic waters. Many species of fish feed off plankton and any interference in its normal manufacture by the oceans would diminish fish supply for countries that depend on it for their day-to-day needs.

The case against the CFCs has become increasingly clear over the past 15 years, demanding a response from the international community. Under the leadership of the United Nations Environment Program, an international Vienna Convention for the protection of the Ozone Layer was adopted. Under the provisions of the Convention, the parties are obligated to cooperate in conducting research and scientific analyses on a number of things—among them the physical and chemical processes that may affect the ozone layer and how changes in the ozone layer may affect the climate. They will also look for alternative substances and technologies.In addition to the Vienna Convention, the Montreal Protocol (a treaty) was negotiated in 1987. By this treaty the major industrial countries agreed to reduce CFC production 50 percent by 1998.

The ozone threat has since grown more serious. The hole in the layer that appears over the Antarctic each summer shows signs of emerging in the Arctic as well, threatening Northern Europe. A NASA survey of ground and satellite data suggested the global ozone layer has thinned by 3 percent in the last 20 years, a faster rate of the destruction than expected. These new data persuaded industrial countries, led by the European Community and the United States, to phase out CFCs entirely by the year 2000. An agreement to this effect was approved by 93 nations in June 1990. A special fund has been set up to assist the developing countries' switch from CFCs.

The ozone shield issue is an unusual environmental issue because it potentially affects the well-being of every individual in every country. It is a global problem affecting countries which may not be using the CFCs at all. The costs of phasing out CFCs will be heavy. Since the substitutes will be less efficient insulators and refrigerants, the U.S. may use 3 percent more electricity. But the case against CFCs is so compelling that almost all governments have now agreed to act in the common interest.

Air Pollution

While Congress contented itself with extending the Clear Air Act of 1970 over the last decade, much of the nation's air kept getting dirtier and half the US population now breathes unhealthy air. But even Congress can't ignore burning lungs forever, and recently the House voted overwhelmingly to strengthen the act. Besides mandating reductions in acid rain and airborne toxics, the bill affects what's put into the tanks of America's 178 million vehicles. Trouble is, these provisions may not do enough to clear the air.

The traditional approach has been to force Detroit to clean up what comes out of tailpipes. That strategy worked—sort of. Twenty years after the original Clean Air Act, vehicles spew out 96 percent fewer hydrocarbons and 76 percent less nitrogen oxides (NOXs), which react in sunlight to form smog. But these gains have been swamped by huge increases in the number of cars on the road, up 51 million from 1970 to 1988. As a result cars are still the single largest source of urban carbon monoxide and smog. Congress and the White House therefore decided to take aim not only at exhaust pipes, but at fuel tanks. "The only cost-efficient way to solve the problem," says Charles Gray, who heads the alternative-fuels laboratory at the US Environmental Protection, "is to use fuels that don't produce dirty emissions."

Unfortunately, this painless route to clean air is not too effective. Reformulated gasolines are not entirely clean but significantly cleaner than the existing stuff. And no matter what their oxygen content, all petroleum-based fuels exacerbate the greenhouse effect. "There is just no way to touch that problem with reformulated gas," says James McKenzie of the environmental research group World Resources Institute.

Nothing short of weaning vehicles from petroleum will do much about the eye-watering ozone and choking smog that blight our cities. Growth in auto travel, about 3 percent per year nationally, will quickly offset any gains from new fuels. Even worse, the fuel law may become a detour away from an environmentally sound transportation policy, one mandating urban car pools and expanding mass transit. The new fuels can serve as a bridge between dirty gasoline and such truly clean energy sources as solar electricity and hydrogen. More funding for research into such renewables will be needed for such futuristic technologies to become practical.Only then can we breathe easier about the nation's air.

Energy conservation can help ease air pollution. Greatly increasing automobile fuel economy is the fastest way to slow down the growth of CO_2 pollution because every gallon burned produces 19 pounds of CO_2.

Fossil fuels when burned emit dangerous pollutants—sulfur dioxide (SO_2), nitrogen oxides, and hydrocarbons. When the oxides of sulfur and nitrogen are emitted from the stacks of factories, smelters, and electrical generating plants, they mix in the atmosphere with oxygen and water to form dilute solutions of strong acids. Eventually they fall to earth as rain, snow, or fog or as acidified dry particles. They may be transmitted long distances, frequently across national boundaries, before they come down. Coal-fired power plants are notorious for sulfur dioxide and particulate emissions (a mixture of pollutants in minute solid form). The oxides of nitrogen come from vehicle exhausts as well as industrial stacks.

Damage to lakes from acid depositions is well documented. Evidence also points to acid rain damage to buildings, crops and forests. The damage to forests seems to be attributable to a combination of acid rain and other forms of pollution. It is occurring all over Europe, with one-fifth of the forests now damaged. Over half of the forests in West Germany are affected, and many are dying.

The sulfur dioxide and particulate emissions associated with coal burning can raise the incidence of respiratory diseases such as coughs and colds, asthma, bronchitis, and emphysema. Particulate matter can carry toxic metals deep into the lungs.

One of the worst auto-related pollutants is ozone, the principal ingredient in urban smog. Ozone can cause serious respiratory distress. Other dangerous pollutants spewed by automobiles include nitrogen dioxide, carbon monoxide, lead, and such toxic hydrocarbons as benzene, toluene, xylene, and ethylene dibromide. Each one of these in turn cause a variety of illnesses and health problems.

Obviously no country can solve the problems caused by polluted air by itself. The UN Economic Commission for Europe has made some progress toward curtailing SO_2 emissions. A Helsinki protocol (treaty) in 1985, mandating 30 percent reductions by 1993, was signed immediately by representatives of 19 nations. The US and the United Kingdom held back, pleading scientific uncertainty. The US has used the same reason of scientific uncertainty with Canada and so Canada is moving ahead unilaterally to cut in half its own SO_2 pollution by 1994.

Air pollution is not high on the list of most people as the world's top killer, but it is truly a global public-health emergency. United Nations statistics show that more than one billion people—a fifth of humanity— live in areas where the air is not fit to breathe. It has become both a rural and an urban problem that crosses the international boundaries as well.

In the United States alone, roughly 150 million people live in areas whose air is considered unhealthy by the Environmental

Protection Agency (EPA). According to the American Lung Association, this leads to as many as 120,000 deaths each year.

Automobiles and industries are the primary cause of air pollution now in most places. In much of Eastern Europe and China coal continues to be the main source of pollution. Adding to the problem, industries are emitting pollutants of frightening toxicity. Millions of tons of carcinogens, mutagens, and poisons pour into the air each year, damaging health and habitat near their sources and, via the winds, sometimes thousands of miles away. Many regions that have enjoyed partial success combating pollution are finding their efforts overwhelmed as populations and economies grow, bringing in more power plants, home furnaces, factories, and motor vehicles.

Global warming has arisen as the preeminent environmental concern, but that should not minimize the importance of the air pollutants because both the air pollutants and the greenhouse gases stem largely from fossil fuels burned in energy, transportation, and industrial systems. Common roots should lead to common solutions but policymakers seem to persist in tackling them separately. This approach runs the risk of lessening one while exacerbating the other. Turning the corner on air pollution requires moving beyond patchwork, end-of-tail pipe approaches to confronting pollution at its sources. This will mean reorienting energy, transportation, and industrial structures toward prevention.

For Reflection and Group Discussion

Human Degradation of Creation (Chapters 5-9)

Chapters 5-9 detail a number of specific environmental problems. Plan ahead now so that you can cover these chapters in a way that is stimulating and appropriate to your group. Consider assigning several persons to each chapter and have them scout out the local angle on their topic and/or write for more information from sources listed in the appendices. Below are some things to keep in mind as you work through these chapters:

1. What interrelationships do you see?

   Try making a "tinkertoy chart": Draw a circle in the middle of a large sheet of paper. Write "greenhouse effect" or another of the problems listed below in it. Think of as many consequences of this problem as you can (polar melting, for example) and write them in surrounding circles, connected by lines to the central circle. Continue outward in this fashion as you consider what effects your second ring of circles might have—perhaps on your own town or household. When you run out of paper, your chart should look like a tinkertoy structure.

2. What do you believe the church's calling is in the face of the environmental crisis? What gifts does it bring, what form should its involvement take? Prayer and fasting? Lobbying and legislation? Alterations in lifestyle? Education? Compare your priorities.

3. The Christian tradition has often stressed nursing, teaching or pastoring as a calling. Do you see science as a ministry as well? Would your congregation ordain someone to an "ecological ministry" or help fund his/her education?

4. Pay attention to your group's morale as you go along. What empowers you to hope and work for change? What immobilizes and discourages? Where do you find hope, joy, humor, opportunity in the face of crisis?

5. What opportunities for worship spring from these chapters? For example, you might visit the landfill where your garbage is dumped and hold a prayer service there. Or, plan a thanksgiving service in which you thank God for those parts of Creation we are utterly dependent on but never notice. (Even a child could appreciate the ozone layer if you used an umbrella to explain it.) Or, write a series of confessions based on these chapters and make this a regular part of your group time.

6
FORESTS

C hanges in the Earth's vegetation can be expected to influence the carbon dioxide content of the atmosphere. Thus, the massive growth of forests some 200-300 million years ago took carbon dioxide out of the air. Eventually, geological transformation of the dying trees and plants converted the carbon into coal, oil, and natural gas. These huge deposits of fossil fuel, the product of millions of years of photosynthesis, remained untouched until coal, and later petroleum and natural gas, were mined and burned, releasing carbon dioxide into the atmosphere. The amounts of these fuels burned to provide human society with energy represent the carbon captured by photosynthesis over millions of years. By burning fossil fuels in the last 750 years we have returned carbon dioxide to the atmosphere thousands of time faster than the rate at which it was removed by the early tropical forests. The atmosphere's carbon dioxide content has increased by 20 percent since 1850, and there is good evidence that the Earth's average temperature has increased about 1 degree Fahrenheit since then.

Deforestation

The destruction of the world's forests is one of the major concerns of our age. People are deforesting the earth—maybe as much as 1.7 billion acres of forest cover has been lost. That destruction continues today, with the tropical zones being the hardest hit and most environmentally critical in terms of global impact. Each year the world loses some 37 million acres of forests. According to United Nations' estimates, almost 40 percent of Central America's forests were destroyed between 1950 and 1980. During the same period, Africa lost 23 percent of its forests and the Himalayan watershed 40 percent. Among the agents of the devastation are inefficient commercial logging operations and the conversion of forested areas to cattle ranching and agriculture through approved governmental policies.

Deforestation takes place when economic and social systems place increasing pressure on the natural resource base which supports them. Fundamentally, these pressures are rooted in rising populations and rising incomes, the former driving the need for agricultural land and wood for energy and shelter, and the latter for forest products to meet consumer demands. With few exceptions, populations in tropical countries are growing between 2 and 3.5 percent per year.

Conversion of forestland to cropland is by far the leading direct cause of tropical deforestation. Such conversion is often necessary since agriculture is clearly the most beneficial use of land in some areas. The tragedy in the tropics is that increasingly the forest is cleared by landless peasants with no alternative for a sustainable lifestyle and it is happening either on land too infertile to sustain crop production over the long term or in a manner that prematurely depletes the land's productive capacity. Meanwhile, cattle ranchers burn and clear at least 2.5 million hectares (a hectare is equal to 2.47 acres) of forest in Central America and Amazonia each year, mainly to raise beef for export to the developed world. And small-scale cultivators, who are denied access to land for subsistence farming elsewhere, cause the final elimination of at least 5 million hectares of forest each year, and gross degradation of another 10 million.

The problems associated with deforestation include depletion of firewood supplies, severe flooding, accelerated loss of soil, encroaching deserts, and declining soil productivity. In many parts of the developing world these problems have assumed disastrous proportions. Firewood is still the primary source of energy for 2 billion people, or three-quarters of the population of the developing world. Fuelwood shortage plagues 57 developing countries, adversely affecting more than a billion people. Torrential rains pouring down deforested Himalayan slopes kill thousands in India and Bangladesh. Denuded Nepal's biggest export is its soil, which through the rivers ends up in the Indian ocean. Many scientists suspect that the spread of the Sahara Desert and the resulting famine in countries of Western Africa have been brought about, at least partially, by deforestation. A further consequence of rapid deforestation can be seen in Haiti, where a continual decrease in the amount of arable land has resulted in smaller harvests even as the population grows—no doubt a prescription for disaster.

The worst has yet to come. If the current rate of deforestation continues unabated, much of the world's remaining tropical forests will disappear by the year 2000, and with them, many of the earth's plants and animals. The loss of these forests will create an energy crisis for 2 billion human beings who will lack sufficient quantities of wood with which to cook their meals and heat their dwellings. In their desperate search for fuel, they will destroy more distant forests, thereby accelerating erosion, changes in climate, and loss of fertile land. Widespread famine may result.

People living in the developed world face an equally catastrophic future if worldwide deforestation continues. New research suggests that the loss of forests aggravates the greenhouse effect, which is caused by burning fossil fuels that emit carbon dioxide. Leaves of trees, on the other hand absorb carbon dioxide, removing it from the atmosphere. When carbon dioxide builds up in the atmosphere, it retains solar heat that would otherwise escape, resulting in global warming. Adapting to such global climatic change will prove costly, especially for the mid-latitude regions of the Northern Hemisphere, where drying trends would severely cut crop yields.Furthermore, the cure for dreaded diseases such as AIDS and cancer, may reside in some plant as yet undiscovered that grows in the rain forest—if destroyed, humankind will be forever denied such help.

If the global climatic change brings any lesson home again, it is the lesson that we are all passengers on the same earth. If global warming, aggravated by tropical deforestation, destroys agriculture in parts of the United States, inundates our coastal areas, and kills millions of acres of our forests, the distinction between "us" and "them" won't matter much. If the tropical forests go, we all lose.

Rain Forests

Rain forests fill the lowland tropics with a luxuriant mantle that rings the globe at the equator, wherever rainfall and temperatures remain high and relatively constant. They include evergreen rain forests (two-thirds of the total), where precipitation is distributed evenly throughout the year, and seasonal forests, where there are at least two dry months.

These forests cover just 7 percent of the planet's land area, but their importance to the biosphere is disproportionate. With warm, wet conditions nearly year-round, growing seasons never stop. Tropical forests serve as a gigantic storehouse for carbon. As whole tracts are cleared and burned, they release more carbon dioxide into the atmosphere, where it traps heat, adding to global warming. Tropical deforestation, ecologists estimate, contributes between 7 and 31 percent of the carbon dioxide humanity releases into the atmosphere each year. The destruction of virgin rain forests probably accounts for nearly half of that amount. The remainder comes mostly from the clearing of regrown "secondary" forests and the more widely spaced trees of open woodlands.

We are only beginning to appreciate the immense value of the extraordinary diversity and richness of the species masked inside the vast scale of these forests. Rain forests are home to half of all species on earth, most of which are still undiscovered, unstudied and unnamed. Biologists do not know whether humans share the earth with 3 million or 30 million living species, nor how many species have been lost already. (See the section on Species Extinction.)

Recent findings prove deforestation is progressing far more rapidly today. According to satellite images analyzed by the Brazilian National Institute of Space Research, 20 million acres of virgin Brazilian forest, an area the size of Maine, went up in smoke in 1987 alone, four times the annual loss previously estimated for Brazil. In 1988 the burning accelerated even more. Photographs taken in 1987 from the US space shuttle *Discovery* revealed a cloud of smoke over the Amazon basin that would have almost covered India. The Brazilian government has since begun to curb deforestation but according to a recent World Resource Institute study, the destruction of the Brazilian rain forests continues at a significant rate and deforestation elsewhere is increasing.

The 1987 data gathered by the World Resource Institute indicate that 11 countries experienced 82 percent of that year's tropical deforestation: Brazil, Indonesia, Burma, India, Colombia, Ivory Coast, Thailand, Laos, Philippines, Nigeria and Vietnam.

As a result of deforestation, Brazil in 1987 caused 1.2 million tons of carbon to be released, about the same amount of carbon released by the United States from the burning of fossil fuels that year, the World Resource Institute study claims.

The depletion of the forests denies subsistence to indigenous populations who are displaced from their forest homes—people who have depended on the forest for basic sustenance. The ecological wisdom of rain forest people dwarfs the scientific knowledge of tropical biologists and botanists. The Kayapo, one of the Amazon's hundreds of endangered Indian tribes, provide a rare, well-documented inventory of indigenous knowledge. American anthropologist Darrell Posey reports that the tribe makes use of 250 types of wild fruit, hundreds of nut and tuber species, and perhaps thousands of medicinal plants. They cultivate 13 distinct bananas, 11 kinds of manioc (cassava), 16 sweet potato strains, and 17 different yams. Many of these varieties are unknown to non-Indians.

U. S. Forests

In the United States, 70 percent of the nation's forests are owned privately and the rest (the 191 million acre national forest system) are owned by the federal government. Environmentalists contend that 95 percent of America's virgin forests have been cut down, the pace of destruction quickened by mechanization and automation. Replanting of trees has been taking place but that creates a uniform "tree farm" with none of the biological diversity of a real forest. It is important to remember that the eastern region of the United States once was covered with dense forests. Westward to about the 95th meridian, beyond the Mississippi River, mighty trees covered the land, save in what are now Illinois and Iowa. As the nation developed into an agricultural-industrial colossus, the destruction of the Eastern forests rapidly proceeded.

Now there is little left of the vast tree cover that once stretched from the Atlantic to the Mississippi and beyond; and only on the Pacific Slope are ancient or "old growth" forests in sizeable tracts still to be found in this country. Because private foresters cut down their tall timber long ago, most of the centuries-old forests are on federal land. Some trees are a thousand years and more old, making them the oldest living things on earth. The old trees of the America's only temperate rain forests are estimated to be vanishing at the rate of 170 acres a day and could be gone in 20 to 30 years.

The old-growth forest in the US is important to the native people of the Pacific Northwest, for it contains critical spawning habitat for the Pacific salmon. Destruction of this habitat, and of the wild runs of salmon, will destabilize Indian communities in the region.

Old-growth forests also represent an irreplaceable religious resource to the Native American community. Native American traditional leaders have identified more than 450,000 acres in the Mount Baker-Snoqualmie National Forest used for spirit-questing, cleansing, gathering medicines and depositing traditional regalia. Most of these sites were in old-growth forest stands.

In relation to forests, the United States has done throughout its history what a righteous world denounces Brazil for doing today; no wonder Brazilian leaders point to the United States as their role model in deforestation. And even without Brazil's development needs, the US continues to clear away its most valuable forests.The United States continues to lecture Brazil on its continuing destruction of its tropical forests. However, it has not taken good care of its own tropical forests in Hawaii and Puerto Rico. To preach respect for nature to Brazil, Americans need to practice it more assiduously in their own forests.

Less than a quarter of Hawaii's original forests remain. At lower levels almost all native plant communities have been destroyed by land-clearing. The loss of habitat has driven 40 percent of Hawaii's native bird species into extinction and threatens three-quarters of those that remain. Predation by introduced species is another source of destruction. Imported vines and grasses suffocate the plants that evolved without competition.

Most of the tropical forest in Puerto Rico seen by Columbus in 1493 has been cleared for farming and housing. But a large national forest and 14 forests managed by Puerto Rico still preserve 3,000 plant species and 232 species of birds. These forests constitute only 4 percent of the island's area but are gradually expanding as agriculture diminishes.

The destruction of the U.S. temperate rain forests is also a major contributor to global warming. Waste generated in timbering, milling, and pulping is burned. The burning results in the freeing of millions of pounds of carbon as carbon dioxide. This carbon is held in place by the trees in temperate forests for hundreds of years. An article in the February 1990 issue of the

Science magazine estimated that 2 percent of global warming is caused by the destruction of the Pacific Northwest forests.

Species Extinction

We are witnessing one of the most remarkable biological phenomena ever to overtake life on earth. A single species, our own, is eliminating the planet's genetic stock. It is happening more rapidly than at any time in the past, except possibly for rare occasions of geologic cataclysm when a mass extinction has depleted the earth's biotas. By the middle of the next century the earth seems likely to lose at least a fourth, probably a third, perhaps half and conceivably a still larger part of the millions of species that inhabit it. It is all happening in the space of just a few decades, the twinkling of an evolutionary eye.

What is the abundance and variety of species that make up the earth's biodiversity? Although we know there are millions of species, we have documented only 1.7 million. Informed estimates tell us there must be at least five million; recent research suggests there could be as many as 30 million insect species in tropical forests alone. We also know that the distribution of species worldwide is far from even. At least two-thirds of them and perhaps as many as 90 percent are concentrated in the Tropics.

Humankind is also reducing the genetic diversity of the planet through selective breeding. Even though the species are not being endangered in terms of their overall numbers, many of them, such as corn, rice and wheat, are suffering a critical decline in their genetic variety.

How fast are the species disappearing? The "background rate" of extinctions during the past 600 million years or so (since multicellular life appeared) has worked out to a rough average of only one per year. The present human-caused rate is at least 1,000 times as great—and may soon become much greater still.

Although it affects many areas, biodepletion is nowhere more rapid than in tropical forests. These forests, although they cover only 7 percent of the earth's surface, shelter at least 50 percent of all species. By early in the next century there could be little left of this biome.

The proximate cause of the loss is the growing number of impoverished forestland farmers. Consider Rondonia, a state in the southern sector of Brazilian Amazonia. Since 1975 the human population there has grown from 111,000 to well over a million. In 1975 only 1,250 square kilometers of forest land had been cleared, but by 1987 the amount had expanded to almost 60,000 square kilometers; three times as large an area has been severely degraded.

The mass demise of species would have immediate economic consequences, some of which could be serious indeed. In 1970 a leaf fungus blighted US cornfields from the Great Lakes to the Gulf of Mexico. America's great Corn Belt almost came unbuckled. The disease eliminated 15 percent of the entire crop, pushing up corn prices by 20 percent and causing losses of more than $2 billion. The situation was saved thanks to blight-resistant germ plasm whose genetic ancestry traces back to variants of corn from one of the plant's native habitat in Mexico. When extinction reduces the Earth's gene pool, remaining life becomes more vulnerable to disease and disaster.

Wild plants also contribute to our health needs. Half of the purchases in the neighborhood pharmacy, whether drugs or pharmaceuticals, derive from wild organisms. The full commercial value of these wildlife-based products worldwide is some $40 billion a year. How many more such opportunities lie hidden in the earth's genome? Investigators have taken a look at only 10 percent of all plant species and have examined only 1 percent of them intensively.

On top of these material benefits, species supply many ecosystem services. They help to maintain the quality of the atmosphere, control climate, regulate freshwater supplies, generate soils, recycle nutrients, dispose of wastes and control pests and diseases. Biodiversity is the reason humans have pharmaceuticals, foods, fibers, sources of oil and ways to regenerate soil.

Whether it is desert plants threatened by motor cycle races or the red squirrels of Arizona's Mount Graham threatened by the proposed construction of an observatory, biodiversity matters because plants and animals contain genetic material. A large gene pool provides the flexibility that natural systems need to reproduce and adapt over evolutionary times.

The impending mass extinction of species is only a part of the story. A longer-term and ultimately more serious repercussion could stem from the disruption of the course of evolution itself. The bounce-back time after a mass-extinction episode has generally been a few million years. The evolutionary outcome this time could be more drastic stretching the bounce-back period to last for many more millions of years.

Species extinction is related to agriculture, industry, technology and trade; to energy and economic growth; population and climate change. It is a problem that requires planning and public policy on a broad scale. The outlook for many species remains bleak. Fortunately, a surge of citizen interest is nudging world governments to work at safeguarding biodiversity and relating it to other environmental issues.

7
WATER
POLLUTION

Water is the precious resource upon which terrestrial life depends for sustenance. Yet, human beings have neglected to maintain its natural reservoirs and safeguard its purity. Agriculture and industries cannot survive without water. Neither can the human body, which is 71 percent water.

The total volume of water on Earth is about 1,400 million cubic kilometers. More than 97 percent is sea water. Of the 3 percent that is fresh water, less than 1 percent is surface water available for human use. Of the rest, some is ground water but most is locked away in snow and ice. The amount available for humans, however, is bountiful for needs if it is managed carefully. The issue confronting us today is the quality of water. Our bodies require water of high quality which nature provides. When humans upset, disrupt, or alter the chemical composition of water in the hydrological cycle, all life forms, not just humans, are in jeopardy.

Groundwater

The balances and cycles of nature keep the total quantity of water in the world essentially constant. Its availability is continuously renewed by nature's water cycle: evaporation, of which 86 percent is from the oceans; rain and snow, with more falling on land than is evaporated from it; and run-off in rivers back to the oceans.

Water is unevenly distributed. The Congo-Zaire basin, for example, has less than 10 percent of Africa's population but more than 50 percent of its water.

Averaged globally, 73 percent of fresh water withdrawn from the earth goes for agriculture (irrigation), 21 percent is used by industry, and 6 percent for domestic consumption. Dramatic increases in crop yields have come from irrigation. At the same time, poorly planned and managed irrigation systems have led to waste that can be ill-afforded. Frequently as much as 70 percent of water used never reaches the crops. Improper drainage leads to salt concentration in the top soil which ultimately makes the land unfit for crop production.

In much of the western US, irrigation is essential for high yields. In the country as a whole irrigated acreage has tripled since 1940. It now accounts for nearly one fourth of the value of the nation's crops. However, underground water reserves have been tapped for irrigation to the point that the Ogallala aquifer, a vast underground lake that spans eight states could disappear by the year 2000. The Ogallala aquifer is being pumped out 20 times faster than it is recharging itself. Extensive irrigation is a major area of concern.

America depends upon plentiful and safe supplies of groundwater. More than 13 million private wells and 100,000 public supply sources pump groundwater to 123 million Americans. But our groundwater has become contaminated by seepage from underground chemical storage tanks and landfills. More than 200 organic and inorganic chemicals have been identified in various groundwater supplies. In addition, more than 700 chemicals have been detected in the US drinking water, 129 of which the Environmental Protection Agency calls dangerous, including industrial solvents, metals and radioactive substances. Americans are so worried about the safety of their drinking water that in 1988 they bought $2 billion worth of bottled water and spent $265 million more for purifying equipment and services. Sales of bottled water and purification devices are expected to increase by 50 percent over the next five years.

In Europe there is great concern over high levels of nitrate in the drinking water due to run-off contaminated by agricultural fertilizers. Nitrate is harmful to young children at excessive levels.

In highly industrialized countries, industry accounts for 60 to 80 percent of total water withdrawals and industries pollute the water more than agriculture. After being used for cooling, cleaning, and processing, more than 80 percent is returned to its source; and thereby all too frequently the by-products or wastes of manufacturing are carried as pollutants to lakes and streams.

Because they often serve as boundary markers, rivers and their associated watersheds frequently fall under the jurisdiction of several, possibly hostile states. An estimated 40 percent of the world's population depends for drinking water, irrigation, or hydropower on the 214 major river systems shared by two or more countries; 12 of these waterways are shared by five or more nations.

Conflicts over water use and quality simmer in virtually all parts of the world, but especially where water resources need to be shared equitably. About 80 countries are already suffering serious water shortages. Disputes center on water diversion, industrial and agrochemical pollution, salinization of streams through heavy irrigation, siltation of rivers, and flooding.

In the Rhine Valley, for example, 20 million people in several countries, but particularly in the Netherlands, must have their drinking water filtered to remove heavy metals, hazardous chemicals, and salt deposited further upstream in France, Switzerland and West Germany. The situation was most extreme following an accident at Sandoz, Inc.'s chemical facilities near Basel, Switzerland, in November 1986. Large amounts of fungicides and mercury spilled into the river, forcing a three-week ban on the use of Rhine water for drinking.

Groundwater Quantity and Quality in the United States

Agriculture is largely responsible for quantity and quality problems in the nation's groundwater. Pumping groundwater for irrigation use has resulted in significant drawdown problems in many aquifers. To the extent that water is recharged to aquifers in agricultural areas, it may carry with it nitrates, pesticides, salts, bacteria, and other dissolved contaminants that potentially could cause serious groundwater pollution problems. Of these, nitrogen fertilizers and soluble pesticides appear to represent the greatest threats.

Pesticides: Modern agriculture has become increasingly dependent on the use of pesticides to protect crops from insects, diseases, weeds, and other threats. Some 50,000 different pesticides products, using 700 active ingredients, are registered for use in the United States. Many of these are suspected carcinogens.

More than one billion pounds of pesticides are used annually in the US. Of the total amount used, only 10 percent is estimated to reach its target. The rest is scattered in soil and water, and carried off by wind.

Over the past 20 years, production and use of chemicals have increased substantially. Herbicide use has grown the fastest. About 85 percent of the herbicides and 70 percent of the insecticides used in US agriculture are applied to only four crops: corn, cotton, soybeans, and wheat. About 25 percent of all pesticides used in 1985 were applied to non-agricultural purposes such as lawn care and wood preservatives.

Evidence of pesticide contamination of groundwater is mounting as well. Recent information indicates that at least 17 pesticides have been found in groundwater in 23 states as a result of agricultural practices. Soluble pesticides and pesticides designed to kill soil pests have the greatest probability to contaminate groundwater.

Fertilizers: Three basic fertilizers are applied to crops: nitrogen, phosphate, and potash. Nitrogen fertilizers account for half of the total and are the only type of fertilizer that seriously contaminates groundwater. In addition to farming, large amounts of chemical fertilizers are also applied in suburban areas on lawns, gardens, and golf courses.

The historical and continued use of nitrogen fertilizers in particular threatens groundwater supplies in much of the United States. Numerous studies demonstrate a relationship between nitrate concentrations in groundwater and nitrogen fertilization rates or fertilization history. About 34 states have reported known contamination of groundwater by nitrates and 4 others reported suspected contamination. The continued buildup of nitrate reservoirs in soils raises concern about future groundwater threats. The threat is most serious for rural America where 90 percent of the population depends on groundwater for drinking.

Oceans and Coastal Areas

The health of the world's oceans, sea and coastal areas is vital to the Earth's well-being. The oceans, which some have called the *lungs* of the planet, cover 70 percent of the Earth's surface and are crucial to the global water cycle. The eco-systems of the oceans are continuous—actually making one world ocean interspersed with land masses. Through scientific research we have begun to learn more about the oceans. We do know that it is a rich and fertile realm of minerals and living creatures useful to humans and magnificent in their own right.

More than two-thirds of the world's population live within 50 miles of a coast, and nearly half of the world's major cities are built on or near an estuary. The coastal zone has the highest biological productivity: some 90 percent of the marine fish harvest is caught within 200 miles of the coast and coastal aquaculture is an increasingly important food source.

Coastal zones connect four identifiable ecosystems that are vital for both humankind and marine life: salt marshes, the tidal wetlands of temperate zones; mangroves, their shrubby tropical equivalents; estuaries, the inlets and ponds where seawater and freshwater intermingle; and coral reefs, teaming with plant and animal life-forms in symbiotic relationships. Coral reefs, mangrove forests and coastal wetlands act as natural barriers against powerful waves and provide essential habitats for many important marine species. At the same time, these systems are extremely vulnerable to the pressures and wastes from human settlements and industries.

About 20 billion tons of waste end up in the sea each year. Coastal waters have been rendered unsafe for swimming, seafood contaminated, and beautiful beaches fouled by garbage including potentially hazardous medical wastes. Coastal habitats are destroyed and populations of marine mammals, fish and shellfish endangered. Coastal settlements everywhere are threatened by the predicted sea-level rise which is expected to result from global warming.

About four-fifths of the pollution that enters the oceans comes from the land—mainly in the form of sewage, industrial waste and agricultural run-off. The other one-fifth comes from coastal mining, energy production and ocean-going vessels, in the form of oil or heavy metals. Almost 90 percent of these contaminants never reach deep water, but have a serious impact on coastal areas. In the United States, two of the greatest ocean "arms"—the Chesapeake Bay on the Atlantic coast and Puget Sound on the Pacific—now require concerted efforts to halt deterioration.

As far away as Antarctica, human-made toxic substances have been detected in deep ocean trenches. The absorptive capacity of oceans is vast, but how much waste they can safely take or the adverse effects of wastes into the future are unknown.

8
WASTE
ACCUMULATION

Solid Waste Disposal

America is a throwaway society. From both industrial and municipal sources, the US generates about 10 billion metric tons of solid waste per year. Every five years the average American discards, an amount of waste equal in weight to the Statue of Liberty.

Americans generate some 160 million tons of municipal trash a year—more than 3.5 pounds for each of us every day—and we are fast running out of places to put it. About 37 percent of this residential and commercial waste is paper. Another 18 percent is yard waste, 8 percent food waste, 10 percent is glass, 10 percent is metals, 7 percent is plastic, and the remainder is wood, rubber, textiles and miscellaneous inorganics. Currently about 6 percent of municipal trash is recycled, 7 percent is incinerated, and 87 percent is disposed in landfills. About 16 billion disposable diapers end up in landfills every year.

Industry produces an additional amount of waste estimated to be as much as 350 million tons per year. A high percentage of the industrial waste is hazardous waste. Most industrial wastes are dumped in private landfills that are unregulated and unmonitored.

Sanitary landfills in the US, a country with abundant land area, have been the preferred method of garbage disposal. Over the years, however, the quality of garbage has changed considerably from primarily kitchen scraps and other organic materials to that which now includes large quantities of paper, plastics, metals, and glass. Toxic household wastes such as old paint thinner or oven cleaner, and pesticides are also part of the garbage which is sent to the landfills.

To address the serious health and environmental threats presented by solid wastes, Congress passed the Solid Waste Disposal Act of 1965, the Resource Recovery Act of 1970, and the Resource Conservation and Recovery Act in 1976.

Plastics

The disposal of plastic waste presents special problems. Some 20 billion pounds of plastics now find their way into the US waste system each year and pile up on roadsides, in the ocean and in landfills. Each American annually uses almost 200 pounds of plastic, roughly 60 pounds of it for packaging. Plastics serve us sometimes for a few hours or weeks but are likely to last several hundred years, because the plastic material resists the degrading action of sunlight and bacteria. Plastic objects do not rust, rot, dissolve or evaporate. By weight, eight percent and by volume, 20 percent of solid waste in American landfills consists of plastic materials.

The National Academy of Sciences has estimated that commercial fishing fleets each year dump at least 52 million pounds of packaging material into the sea and lose some 300 million pounds of indestructible plastic fishing lines and nets. The resulting annual death toll, experts say, from plastic fishing gear, six-pack yokes, sandwich bags and styrofoam cups amounts to one to two million seabirds and 100,000 marine mammals (including whales and seals with intestinal blockages caused by plastic bags) and countless fish. The Marine Sciences Research Center at Stony Brook, L.I., has estimated that 30 percent of the fish in the world's oceans have tiny pieces of plastic in their stomachs that interfere with digestion.

When incinerated, chlorine-based plastics contribute to the formation of dioxins and furans. Some of these molecules are considered highly toxic and are implicated in weakening the immune system, affecting fetal development and causing a skin disorder called chloracne.

A study prepared for the Society of the Plastics Industry estimates that the use of plastics in food packaging will double between 1985 and 2000. By the turn of the century, annual US resin production for all uses will reach 76 billion pounds. Plastics will then be a $345-billion industry employing 1.5 million people in 28,000 firms.

Unfortunately plastic makes inroads at the expense of easily recycled glass and aluminum. The soft drink industry presents one of the leading examples of the shift to plastic containers. Two-liter plastic bottles were introduced in 1978 and now carry 22 percent of the soft drink volume sold in the US. By weight, several times more plastic is now produced in the US than aluminum and all other nonferrous metals combined.

Plastic sales have grown at an annual rate of almost 5 percent since 1977. Bottlers of ketchup, canners of soup, and packages of laundry detergent are all adopting lightweight, unbreakable—and non-biodegradable —plastic containers.

Disposing of used plastic wastes enormous amounts of energy. According to Dr. Jack Milgrom, a plastic analyst, "Recycling plastics saves twice as much energy as burning them in an incinerator. Producing a fabricated plastic product from scrap instead of virgin resin saves some 85 to 90 percent of the energy otherwise used, including the energy of the petroleum feedstocks [derivatives] used to manufacture the resin."

In 1987, the US used almost one billion barrels of petroleum—enough to meet the nation's demand for imported oil for five months—just to manufacture plastics.

Recycling of plastics is difficult because more than 46 resins are in common use—in different combinations— to make different kinds of plastics. And the recycling processes can handle only one type of plastic.

Hazardous Waste

Apart from municipal waste, the chemical and manufacturing industries in the US generate about 260 million tons of hazardous (toxic) waste each year, about one ton for every man, woman and child. The growing amounts of toxic waste largely coincide with the expansion of the chemical industry between 1945 and 1970 when the production of synthetic chemicals increased tenfold.

The problem of toxics is the problem of synthetic chemicals.The petrochemical industry has had a phenomenal growth ever since the stimulus of wartime shortages during World War II. It is based on the properties of carbon, which laboratory scientists have learned to exploit not only to recreate chemicals found in nature, but also to manufacture an endless number of synthetic chemicals that were never present in nature—fibers, pesticides, pharmaceuticals, and an unlimited variety of plastics.

Worldwide, some 70,000 chemicals are now in everyday use, and anywhere from 500 to 1,000 new ones are put into use each year. Production has been doubling every eight years and no limit to the number of possible syntheses is in sight. Many of the chemicals are toxic. Toxic materials are used in their manufacture and toxic wastes are generated as by-products of manufacture.

Intrusion into an ecosystem of substances wholly foreign to it may result in environmental degradation. For example, synthetic plastic unlike natural materials, is not degraded by biological decay. It therefore persists as rubbish or is burned—in both case causing pollution. In the same way, a toxic substance such as DDT or lead, which plays no role in the chemistry of life and interferes with the actions of the substances that do, is bound to cause ecological damage if sufficiently concentrated. In general, any productive activity which introduces substances foreign to the natural environment runs a considerable risk of polluting it.

Until about a decade ago, the primary solution for disposal of toxic waste was to bury 50 gallon drums of waste in landfills, or to dump it into pits, lagoons, or wells. As public awareness of the danger of toxic chemicals spread, new laws were passed by Congress to control their use and disposal.

The Resource Conservation and Recovery Act (RCRA) was passed in 1976 to address growing problems with disposal of both solid and hazardous wastes. The Toxic Substance Control Act (TSCA) was also passed at this time to regulate toxic chemicals throughout their manufacture, use and disposal cycles. Monitoring and research under these laws helped reveal the extent of toxic waste contamination the nation faced.

Once the magnitude and severity of the hazardous waste disposal problem was revealed, Congress passed the Comprehensive Environment Response Compensation and Liability Act—Superfund, a five-year $1.6 billion project, which outlined a plan of action for the cleanup of the nation's worst hazardous waste sites.

Synthetic chemicals pose great risks and perhaps cause thousands of deaths each year in the U.S. In the short run, it is hard to demonstrate with certainty the impact pesticides and a broad range of chemicals are capable of producing in those who come in contact with them. It often takes 20 to 40 years for exposure to these chemicals to lead to the appearance of the disease or its adverse effects on human and other lives. However, it is still clear that many of these chemicals are dangerous.

9
MISUSE
OF LAND

Human beings depend on the earth's crustal surface for just about all of their life-sustaining needs. The land is extremely versatile. It produces our food, provides our basic fuels and metals, and supports our steel and concrete structures and buildings. Protection of our land resources is crucial to the welfare of humankind.

The thinnest part of the earth's surface, the soil is a recent addition in the planet's history. From it come most of our necessities. Land is essentially a non-renewable resource because nature's manufacture of soil requires centuries to complete. Food, like water, is an absolute necessity. Without arable land human beings could not live. However, soil erosion and relentless desertification are destroying our productive land. Deforestation also is a contributing factor to land degradation (see the section on Forests).

Soil Erosion

Soil erosion is slowly undermining the productivity of one-third of the world's cropland. Between 1950 and 1984, the world grain harvest expanded some 2.6 times, or nearly 3 percent per year, raising per-capita grain production by more than one-third. But in the last half decade since, output rose only 0.2 percent per year. This five-year period is obviously too short to show a trend, but it does suggest an unsettling slowdown in food output, one that is partly due to environmental degradation.

According to Lester Brown of the Worldwatch Institute, "Among the environmental trends adversely affecting agriculture, soil erosion tops the list." As the demand for food has risen in recent decades, so have the pressures on the earth's soils. Soil erosion is accelerating as the world's farmers are pressed into plowing highly erodible land, and as traditional rotation systems that maintain soil stability break down.

Some one-third of the world's cropland is losing topsoil at a rate that undermines its future productivity. An estimated 24 billion tons of topsoil washes or blows off the land annually— roughly the amount on Australia's wheatland. Each year, the world's farmers must try to feed 88 million more people with 24 billion fewer tons of topsoil.

On an average, cropland in the United States loses 4.4 tons of top soil per acre annually. Top soil is the matrix of all of our lives—the lives of the plants, the animals who live on the land and eat the plants, and the humans who eat both the animals and the plants. It takes God and nature ten thousand years to produce one inch of top soil, and the typical agricultural region contains only six inches of this precious gift. If we continue this abuse of the land, in fifteen years, the planet's fertile lands will be reduced by one-third.

Farming done on too large a scale, and in too mechanized a fashion, inevitably degrades the layer of rich and fertile earth that is America's greatest single asset. Most American farmers today cannot produce a bushel of corn without sending a bushel of topsoil floating down the Mississippi. This sort of degradation is nearly irreversible under the present US system, because too few people are farming—only about 2 percent of the US population. With such a small number of people involved in farming, the care and the highly localized skill needed to protect and nourish the soil is impossible when a single farmer, riding high in the cab of a modern tractor, must tend hundreds of acres.

Around the world the situation in many places is much worse. Roughly half of all countries and half of all arable lands are suffering from erosion at unacceptable levels. If this continues unchecked, it will offset all the new land likely to be brought under cultivation by the year 2000. Guatemala has lost 40 percent of its lands productive capacity. In Turkey, 54 percent of the land is severely eroded. Haiti has no top quality soil left. One quarter of India's land area suffers significantly from erosion. Once the soil is gone, it is lost forever.

Desertification

One of the most widespread population-related environmental problems is the ecological degradation of Earth's land surface in a process called "desertification." Desertification is a phenomenon of the world's dry lands, which in greater part are more suited to grazing livestock than to growing crops. Salt—salinity— and alkali infestations are still menacing the many populations that live in arid and semi-arid plains and valleys.

In natural dry lands, the water tables are often salty, but stay at greater depths. The soils above are salt-free and support grasses and legumes whose stature is small because of the paucity of water. When irrigation canals are installed, the fresh water gratifyingly escalates the crop yields and the costly enterprise is declared a success.

Over the years, improper drainage, leaks in canals and excessive irrigation send water below the root zone and the groundwater table slowly rises. Long before it reaches the surface, the wicklike suction of the soil will have accumulated enough salt to kill all crops. White salt incrustations, black blotches of alkali humus, and scattered, salt-tolerant bushes and herbs take over. The dreaded "rise of the alkali" is one of the several human-made forms of desertification.

Where salt and soil chemistry are compatible and suitable topographies prevail, reclamation of sands and loams, but rarely of clay soils, have been accomplished in tedious, costly steps.

Desertification is also caused by destruction of vegetation by woodcutting, burning, and overgrazing, by erosion by water and wind as a result of poor land management, and by soil impaction (by cattle hoofs, tractors, drying, and the impact of raindrops on denuded soil surfaces). Its terminal stage is easily recognized—a barren wasteland, virtually devoid of vegetation, familiar to those who have seen TV stories of famine in the Sahel. A functional ecosystem is degraded to the point where it can provide few, if any, services to humanity.

But in its earlier stages, desertification can go unrecognized by most people. For instance, overgrazing has ruined much of the grasslands of the Western United States. Nonetheless the average citizen of, say Albuquerque, New Mexico, does not realize that he or she lives in an area desertified by human action—that the upper Rio Grande Valley was once a rich grassland.

The United Nations Environment Program summarizes the overall desertification issue with the following facts and figures:

- 4.5 billion hectares (1 hectare equals 2.47 acres), or 35 percent of the earth's land surface, are threatened with desertification. They support some 850 million people.

- Of this total—on which a fifth of humanity makes its living—three-fourths has already been moderately degraded and fully one-third has lost more than 25 percent of its productive potential.

- Each year about 6 million hectares of land are irretrievably lost to desertification.

- The rural population affected by serious desertification rose from 57 million in 1977 to 135 million in 1984. Those affected are the ones who can least afford it: people living in low-income developing countries that are climatically, geographically and economically disadvantaged.

- In India, scientists now blame desertification and deforestation for the worsening of droughts and floods.

- In dollar terms, the value of production lost is estimated at $26 billion per year. To halt the deterioration and restore much of the land would cost an estimated $4.5 billion a year. Not much has been done to develop a more appropriate relationship with the land.

PART IV

Other Factors
Impacting
the Creation

10
POPULATION
AND
ENVIRONMENT

At the end of World War II there were about 2.4 billion people in the world. Now there are 5.3 billion. If the current rates of growth continue, (about 1.7 percent annually) nearly a billion more people will be sharing the planet by the year 2000. This is the equivalent of adding a new China.

World population is growing faster than expected. In its latest annual survey made public in May 1990, the United Nations Fund for Population Activities (UNFP) said that the world's population will stabilize at the end of the 21st century at 11.3 billion rather than the 10.2 billion it previously forecast. It warned that without more vigorous efforts to control growth worldwide population might increase to about 14 billion before it stabilized.

With more than 90 percent of the increase concentrated in developing countries, the report says that continuing fast population growth will lead to greater numbers of poor and hungry people. It also means increased damage to the environment from the growing pressure of people on land, forests and water supplies, and with the additional heat that more people create, the risk of climate change.

In many developing countries, soaring population now has a dual effect on food balance: it increases demand as it degrades the agricultural resource base. For instance, crowded cities and villages create a need for firewood that exceeds the sustainable yield of local forests. Deforestation is the outcome, which in turn increases rainfall runoff and soil erosion. Once started, this vicious cycle is hard to stop. As a result, the agricultural base for hundreds of millions of people is deteriorating on a scale whose consequences are fearful to imagine.

Nowhere is the agricultural breakdown more evident than in Africa, which has the fastest population growth of any continent on record. A combination of deforestation, over-grazing, soil erosion, and desertification has helped lower per capita grain production some 20 percent from its peak in the late sixties. This drop has converted the continent into a grain-importing region, fueled the region's mounting external debt, and left millions of Africans hungry and physically weakened.

There are already many places where human concentrations have overwhelmed the ability of the environment to support them at a quality of life that is humane and acceptable. Attention to population growth is necessary to maintain life on planet Earth.

Great inequities in standards of living now exist among the peoples of the world. As a consequence, per capita impact on the Earth's resource base varies dramatically. Americans, constituting five percent of the earth's population, consume approximately 25 percent of the earth's resources. The impact of each American on the earth's resources is many times more than that of a person in a less developed society.

The United States, with the fastest growing population in the industrialized world, also experiences population pressures. The population of Florida is growing faster than that of Kenya, the world's fastest growing nation. As a result, Florida's drinking water supply is in dangerous shape. The population around Chesapeake Bay, the nation's largest and most valuable estuary, increased 50 percent between 1950 and 1980. The result has been increased pollution run-off that has smothered oyster and clam beds, commercial fishing pressure that has almost wiped out the striped bass, and a decline in the quality of the water in the Bay.

There are examples all over the nation of population pressures destroying once productive natural environments. From a global perspective, US population growth has far-reaching effects. Every year, for example, US population growth causes the loss of enough farmland to provide millions of people with a minimum diet.

In their new book, *The Population Explosion,* Paul R. Ehrlich and Anne H. Ehrlich of Stanford University, advance the thesis that we are rushing headlong toward disaster because of over-population. Our numbers are too large in relation to the ecosystem, they argue, and unless interventionist policies are adopted, the global population will soon be subjected to natural forces (perhaps massive increase in death rates) that will bring it back into balance.

The Ehrlichs find evidence for concern in such examples of environmental degradation and resource exhaustion as global warming, acid rain, topsoil erosion, ground water depletion, destruction of the ozone layer, desertification and deforestation. By environmental standards, wealthier countries are at least as guilty of overpopulation as are poorer countries. Although the average birth rate in industrial countries is only 1.9 children per woman, these smaller, more stable populations consume more resources per capita, and they rely on more disruptive technologies. They are more likely, for example, to get about in automobiles than on bicycles.

Environmental degradation is a serious problem. The exhaustion of nonrenewable resources, though the evidence is less clear-cut, may be equally serious. Certainly, the facts on balance seem to indicate that both are worsening. Less obvious, however, is what causes these problems.

We can point to three factors: population (the number of people), level of affluence (how much they consume) and technology (the degree to which their consumption generates environmental degradation). Since the publication of the Ehrlich's "Population Bomb" two decades ago, a debate has raged over which of these factors is most important. Then as now, the Ehrlichs emphasized population. Others, most notably Barry Commoner, have argued that technology is paramount, especially in developed countries like the United States. From a policy perspective, this dispute may be less important than identifying which of the factors can be most easily and rapidly changed.

The continued dangers of environmental degradation suggest that it would be prudent to address the population factor. This is especially true since we have evidence that most of the world's women want to have fewer children than they are at present likely to have. Yet even if replacement-level birth rates were to be reached this year (an impossible goal), the present age structure of the world's population would keep it growing for another 50 to 60 years. What demographers call "population momentum" makes curbing population growth a long range project.

The limitations governing the other factors—affluence and technology—are less clear. The Ehrlichs' argument underestimates the capacity of human institutions and technology to change. Could institutional and technological adaptation occur fast enough to deal with current and prospective problems? It is not easy to know the answer. The experience of the last 20 years is mixed. On the one hand, we have witnessed the results of the green revolution in agriculture and improvements in air quality following the imposition of automotive emission standards. On the other hand, we have seen the discovery of ozone depletion, deforestation and acid rain as major environmental problems.

For Reflection and Group Discussion

1. Choose the environmental problem from chapters 5-9 that bothers you most. How is it related to population growth? How will continued population growth impact this problem?

2. Three factors affect environmental degradation—population, level of affluence and technology. Which do *you* think is most important? Most easily changed?

3. How does this chapter affect your own feeling about having children, if you have not already made this decision?

4. How does this chapter affect your feeling about death? High tech health care? Respond to the Ehrlichs' claim that natural forces (including massive increases in death rates) may be needed to bring global population back into balance.

11
BIOTECHNOLOGY AND CREATION

Genetic Engineering

Over nearly four decades, molecular biologists have made great strides in understanding inheritance. Scientists now understand how genetic information is stored in a cell, how that information is duplicated and how it is passed from cell to cell, generation to generation. The key discovery on the road to the Creation of biotechnology occurred in 1953, when Watson and Crick correctly theorized the structure and operation of the DNA (deoxyribonucleic acid) molecule.

As a result of the work done by Watson and Crick, we now know that DNA molecule is a double helix—two strands of DNA connected by chemicals, called bases. We also know that all DNA in all living cells has a similar structure, function and composition. DNA is present in all living cells. It has been called the "master molecule of life," because it (1) directs the manufacture of proteins which go to make up the body, and (2) it makes a copy of itself (replication) so that each cell will have a complete set of genetic information.

Within the last decade, scientists have discovered how the DNA encodes and passes on genetic characteristics. Once this was known, scientists were able to isolate a specific DNA sequence from one species and *recombine* it with a DNA sequence from another species. Hence the term "recombinant DNA." This breaking and linking of different pieces of DNA is, then, a recombination of genes, and the ability to transfer genetic information is known as "genetic engineering."

Genetic engineering is nothing more than a body of methods, intricate in detail but simple in principle, by which genes or groups of genes are taken from one cell and inserted into another, where they may link up with the genes already there and contribute to the biochemical processes of their host. Donor and host may be of widely different species—rabbit to mouse, say; alfalfa or pig to bacterium. The physical substance of the genes, a stretch of DNA, is picked out, transferred, and integrated into the host—hence the more formal term for the technology, recombinant DNA (rDNA) or popularly, "gene splicing."

Genetic exchange has always happened within nature. It is the method by which we have variations within a given species. Human beings have also sought genetic changes in plants and animals to increase certain desirable traits. This was done by selective breeding and cross-breeding. The results include self-fertilizing crop plants and meatier, faster growing livestock.

What is new with DNA splicing or "genetic engineering" is the ability of scientists to control this process with new speed and new accuracy. Whereas other methods were slow, somewhat random and within the same species, it is now possible to hook together DNAs from different species in a rationally planned way, since bacteria, plants and animals all use the same genetic code. A natural change within a DNA molecule is called mutation. If the mutation occurs in germ cells (the reproductive cell), it is the basis for genetic diseases. If it occurs in the *somatic* cells (the rest of the cells in the body), its effect will be confined to the individual.

The process called recombinant DNA (rDNA), revolutionizes our entire relationship with the natural world. With rDNA technology it is now possible to snip, insert, stitch, edit, program and produce new combinations of living things just as our ancestors were able to heat, burn, melt and solder together various inert materials creating new shapes, combinations and forms.

Genetic engineering is the first way to create new life. It is a staggering idea—a "second big bang," as one biologist put it. There is a certain irony here. Just in time—just as the clouds of carbon dioxide threaten to heat the atmosphere—we are figuring out a new method of domination, a method more thorough, and therefore more promising, than burning coal and oil and natural gas. It is the method that offers us the most hope of continuing our way of life, our economic growth. It promises crops that need little water and can survive the heat; it promises crop plants toxic to insect pests and herbicide tolerant crops; it promises cures for the new ailments we are creating as well as the old ones we have yet to defeat; it promises a way to survive in almost any environment we may create. The development of this technology is the logical outcome of our belief that we must forever dominate the world to our advantage.

Genetic engineering bypasses all the natural constraints we were up against till recently. No longer are we limited to manipulating species through selective breeding; now we can play chemical mix and match games with all of life. For example, in 1983, Harold Brinster of the University of Pennsylvania Veterinary School inserted human growth hormone genes into mice embryo. At birth, the mice expressed the human genes and grew twice as fast and twice as big as any other mice in history. These "super mice," then passed the human growth hormone gene on to their offspring. A strain of mice that have human genes permanently incorporated into their being are now a part of our world.

The "super mice" example illustrates how the new genetic technologies allow us to combine genetic material across natural boundaries turning all of life into manipulable chemical materials. This kind of biological manipulation changes our concept of nature and our relationship to it. For the first time in history humans become the architects of life itself. We become the Creator and designer. We begin to program the genetic codes of living things to suit our own cultural and economic needs. We take on the task of creating a second genesis, a synthetic one, geared up for efficiency and productivity.

The short term benefits of this extraordinary new power are indeed seductive. The economic and commercial possibilities are vast and the benefits to humankind unquestioned. These include the production of human insulin, the potential for vaccines for AIDS and malaria, huge increases in agricultural production and the ability to break down toxic wastes. Yet biotechnology also brings unprecedented concerns.

The concerns have to do with the release and potentially harmful spread of "synthetic" species through the environment, and also the loss of diversity resulting from mass production of crops. The use of biotechnology may have very serious and often unpredictable environmental, social and economic consequences, especially in developing countries. It raises urgent moral and theological questions concerning respect for life and the environment.

Concerns are raised and worries are provoked when scientists speculate about using genetic engineering in the clinic—on human beings. Ethical concern sharpens when the speculation stretches to changing genes or adding them in human germ cell—ova or sperm. Some critics even assert we are in danger of tampering irrevocably with human evolution.

Military Uses of Genetic Engineering

There is growing evidence that biological and chemical warfare research programs around the world are using genetic engineering. Such research programs focus in on "militarily significant" bacteria, viruses, and toxins. These pathogens can be used to destroy animals, crops, and people. They can mutate, reproduce, multiply, and spread over a large geographic area by wind, animal, and insect transmission. Once released, many biological pathogens are capable of not only surviving but also maintaining themselves in the environment indefinitely.

Patenting of Animals in the US

For the purposes of the United States Patent and Trademark Office (P.T.O.), all life can now be regarded as a "manufacture or composition of matter." If a researcher implants a foreign gene into an animal's genetic code—for example a human growth hormone gene into a pig—the genetically altered animal is considered a human invention, like a toaster, automobile or a tennis ball.

The US patent policy thus transforms the status of the biotic community from common heritage to the private preserve of major corporations and it provides the necessary government guarantee that the raw materials of the biotechnology age, that is, all living things on the planet can now be exploited for commercial gain by chemical, pharmaceutical and biotechnology companies. The battle to control the gene pool and the genetic age has already begun.

On April 7, 1987, the Patent and Trademark Office issued a policy finding that patents could be granted on genetically-engineered higher life forms. The finding was based on *Diamond* v. Chakrabarty (related to the patenting of oil-eating bacteria) and an April 3, 1987 decision of the Board of Patent Appeals and

Interferences allowing the patenting of sterilized oysters. On April 12, 1988, after nearly three years of consideration, the US Patent and Trademark Office granted a patent to Harvard University on a special mouse developed by Philip Leder and Timothy Stewart. The research was sponsored by DuPont, which therefore owns the patent rights. In the absence of legislation and regulations regarding patentability of genetically-engineered higher life forms, such decisions currently rest on the shoulders of a federal employee at the P.T.O.

What the patent policy suggests is that pigs and primates, dogs and cats, birds and beasts are suddenly reclassified, stripped of their species integrity, robbed of their special biological bonds and reduced to the level of chemical compositions. Even human genetic traits are now patentable and any number of human genes can be transferred to other animals. With the exception of *homo* sapiens, the engineered animals with human genes functioning in their genetic code can be patented. Is all life to be reduced to a manufactured process subject to patenting and ownership by private companies? Or, do living things have the right to be themselves—separate species each with a unique nature—whether or not there is profit in them for humans? In 1988, some church leaders called for a moratorium on animal patenting.

Impact on the Third World

As things stand in our world today, biotechnology is designed primarily to meet the needs of monopolistic and capital intensive economies. Given a necessary profit motive in research and development of related technology, most of this technology is not focused on the needs of nations where the payback is limited. In fact, it could spell even swifter and more widespread deprivation of Third World peoples and their environment.

In agriculture, it has the potential for a massive displacement of traditional agricultural commodities. What consequences will that bring to the Third World producers of such commodities? For example, experiments are in progress that might lead to the production of "natural" vanilla flavor in the laboratory—a process which could eliminate the need for traditional cultivation of vanilla beans. This could result in the loss of over $50 million in annual export earnings for Madagascar where three quarters of the world's vanilla beans are produced.

Cacao butter and sweeteners to replace sugar are other examples of Third World agricultural commodities that are endangered by biotechnological developments.

The whole area of patenting of seeds and plant varieties is likely to take the genetic materials out of the hands of small farmers in the Third World and put them into the hands of transnational agribusiness. The small farmer, as a result, is then at a further disadvantage. Genetic engineering may further reduce the diversity of seeds that have already been depleted by the present methods of crop improvement. For example, in Bolivia and Peru, the number of potato varieties has been reduced from about 6,000 to 300 and it is possible that genetic engineering could reduce it even further.

Comparable impacts may also be felt in the areas of livestock and drugs production.

For Reflection and Group Discussion

1. Respond to the question ending the last paragraph of this chapter. Why should we safeguard the integrity of species? The genetic diversity of species?

2. How is gene splicing different from selective breeding and other forms of species manipulation from the past? Would you describe it as "a second big bang" as this author does?

3. List potential benefits of genetic engineering. List potential negative effects. Which is worse—refusing to use power for a good end or developing and using power which may easily be abused?

4. Biotechnology is only one of several areas where humans now wield "God-like power." How does this power change our relationship to God? To the world?

5. For an ancient example of the way genetic manipulation can be used to benefit one party but not another, see Genesis 30:25-43.

PART V

Economy And Ecology Linkages

12
ECOLOGY, ECONOMY, AND ECONOMIC SYSTEMS

Earlier we observed that the term "ecology" is derived from the Greek *oikos* meaning household or home. The Greek word from which we derive *economy, oikonomia,* is a compound of *oikos,* household, and *nomos,* law or management. Ecology means a study of organisms 'at home,' with everything that affects them. *Economy* means literally "the law or management of the household." In this case, the household is connected with production, distribution, and consumption of the necessities of life and refers to whole economies as households.

Many of the biblical traditions represent God as engaged in creating, sustaining, and recreating households. *Household* can refer to the people of Israel or the church of Jesus Christ, to families, to a royal court or dynasty, to a place of God's abode, or in the most comprehensive sense, to the whole Creation. God has made Godself responsible for the households of Israel and the church, the household of nations, and the household of everything God has brought into being. The *oikonomia tou theou* (economy of God) applies to the life of the Christian community (Col. 1:25; 1 Cor. 9:17; Eph. 3:2; 1 Tim. 1:4) as well as to God's work of salvation for the household of the Creation (Eph. 1:9-10; 3:9-10). Because of the peculiar promises made by this God, the life of God is inextricably connected with the livelihood and future of these households.

Interrelations and Conflicts Between Ecology and Economy

Ecology in essence requires a harmonious living with nature. The components of nature—of ecosystems—are identified as materials that have value and function in their own right as *finished materials*. Economy, as we practice it presently requires a disharmonious consumption of nature. Nature is identified as "raw" material. "Rude resources," "Crude resources," and "Natural resources" are other names we give to nature. Nature is also considered to be the "away" where we put the unwanted things we make—our wastes and discards. Building of depositories for continuous separation of wastes from human producers and consumers is a more recent approach in waste disposal. Unwanted things are thrown "away" or put into places designed to isolate them from ourselves but in nature there is no such thing as "away."

Moreover ecosystems are so arranged that their parts and products are designed to be re-cycled. They are so inter-related—with decomposers, for example—that they are broken down and reprocessed rapidly. Through such "death and decay" springs life. Our economic system also produces things that have their usefulness, but it gives little consideration to re-cyclability. Some things are designed for durability with the inevitable consequence that when thrown "away," they may last a long,long time—accumulating in the depositories designed for them.

Nature is used both directly and indirectly when raw materials are processed for the production of goods, and nature is polluted by the emissions and wastes of this production. In both of these processes, nature remains the loser—exchanging raw materials for the waste that is produced. Besides labor and capital, nature is truly an exploited third factor of production. How can the nature's position in this "game" be improved, its rights guaranteed and its integrity protected?

The conflict between economy and ecology lies primarily in their basic principles: the ecological principle of "*stability,*" and the economic principle of "*growth.*" While ecological systems depend on equilibrium for survival, in economic systems, profit depends on expansion. These principles are simply not compatible.

The use of "raw materials" and the generation of "wastes" is an old issue. Technological development has, however, made it increasingly possible to exploit depletable resources, and has led to an increasing accumulation of non-decomposable wastes. Nature is no longer able to absorb all these materials, many of which are not only toxic for nature but for human beings as well.

Efforts to hide emissions and wastes—in dumping sites, in storage places, in water or in the air by building high smokestacks—have proven only temporarily successful. Most pollutants are "mobile poisons"; they do not stop at borders. One result of these procedures of disposal is an interruption of ecological cycles that results in a reduction of the natural diversity, a decline in the robustness of the ecosystems and a breakdown of ecological symbioses and equilibria. As a consequence, the absorption capacity of the natural environment decreases and environmental pollution increases.

The challenge to economic theory and practice lies in the question of whether and how these economic principles can be reshaped in harmony with ecological principles. The answer to this question depends upon two things—one, what really matters to people; and two, their willingness to change. What we need is an economic policy regulated by ecological principles and a "true economy" that is part and parcel of Creation's economy.

Ecological Self-regulation

Certainly, only a small fraction of the environmental problems would exist if the economic contexts would have remained so small that producers and consumers could personally recognize the consequences of depleting resources and polluting nature. In other words, business profitability, economic growth, and the expansion of world markets could not be guaranteed or increased without externalizing some of the given costs. This is called the problem of the external effects of production. For example, cutting down rain forests for farming inflicts costs on the natural flora and fauna that existed there before the destructive human intervention took place.

Science and technology tend to shift the costs of development to third parties, future generations, and nature. Obviously, one solution rests in shifting the costs back to the economic units that cause the problems. Also, all investment decision-making must include the "ecological component." But how to do this in a practical way?

Recycling, in the broadest sense of the term, is an important component of the solution. It would lead to a systematic reduction of the use of the depletable resources, and the generation of polluting wastes. This approach contradicts an economy organized for quick throughput. In practice, recycling is just beginning as a systematic economic undertaking.

Secondly, "ecological accounting" becomes critical. This means taking into consideration the amount of energy, materials, wastes, and land used by a given course of action and providing such information to the public.

Another important ecological principle to keep in mind is the *sustainability* of resource use. A sustainable use of land for agricultural purposes, a sustainable harvest of forest trees and so on, become strategic. Forest owners, traditionally "do not cut more wood than can be regrown." This principle is now challenged by the "acid rain," that originates externally but which affects the yield of forests. Nature fights back in the form of dying trees.

The society also needs to reestablish the principle of *responsibility* or *liability* for environmental problems. The current legal system requires the proof of who caused the damage before determining the liability of the polluting party. In countries like Japan, the statistical probability of being detected is sufficient for obligating polluters to compensate damages. Once this principle was applied, it helped to improve environmental quality through ecological self-regulation of business activities.

Ecological Orientation of Economic Policy

Confronted with serious environmental problems, conventional economic policy is increasingly being challenged. Its guiding principles, goals, instruments, and institutions are being questioned, and a new concept is emerging: *ecological* economic policy.

An ecological economic policy in contrast to the conventional policy would call for changes in the principles that guide the economy, the goals of the economy and the institutions that govern the economy. This is not an easy task but it is a necessary one in view of the life and death questions that a status quo approach to the environment has brought about.

A better harmony between economy and ecology is a tremendous task, conceptually as well as practically, but it offers the only chance to reconcile the interests of human beings and nature.

Ecology and Economic Systems

A vast amount of literature exists on environmental deterioration. Clearly, by far the largest part of the problem has its origin in the world's economy as it has developed in the last three to four centuries. This of course has been the period of the emergence of capitalism, communism, socialism and of the bourgeois and industrial revolutions; of utilitarianism; of coal and steam and railroads, of steel and electricity and chemicals, of petroleum and automobile, of mechanized and chemicalized agriculture—and of the rapid urbanization of the world's population.

All of these developments have put growing pressure on the Earth's resources. They have introduced new methods and substances into the processes of producing, using, and disposing of the worn-out goods. Perhaps there have been cases where these activities were carried out with a view to respecting and preserving the natural cycles. Such instances, if any, have left little trace in the historic record.

Change in the human economy has always originated with individuals or sub-groups hoping for specific benefits for themselves. The indirect effect on the environment did not concern them; or, if they thought about it at all, they took for granted that whatever effects their actions might have would be easily absorbed or compensated for by nature's seemingly limitless resilience.

We know now that such ways of thinking about the processes in question are deceptive. Activities damaging to the environment may be relatively harmless when introduced on a small scale; but when they come into general use and permeate whole economies on a global scale, the problem is radically transformed. This is precisely what has happened in case after case, especially in the half century following the Second World War. The cumulative result is *the* environmental crisis.

We have described the major elements of the crisis in several chapters of this book. We have also explored the interconnections of the various components of the environmental crisis. But the crisis is a radical (and growing) disjunction between the demands placed on the environment by the modern global economy, and the capacity of the natural forces to meet and survive these demands. This is true both in capitalistic or socialistic systems. Recent reports coming out of some of the Eastern European countries portray environmental degradation that is almost unbelievable.

What Needs to Happen?

Some of what needs to happen has been discussed above under the ecological economic policy and ecological self-regulation matters. We now operate under a global economy in which capital plays an important role. The development and application of science to industry and agriculture have progressed beyond anyone's wildest dreams a hundred and fifty years ago. Despite all the dramatic changes, however, the system remains what it was at its birth, a juggernaut driven by concentrated energy of individuals and small groups pursuing their own self-interests, checked only by their mutual competition. They are controlled in the short run by the impersonal forces of the market and in the longer run, when the market fails, by devastating crises. It is fueled by conversion of what for centuries was considered to be a *vice* into *virtue:* human greed. "Looking out for number one" no longer refers to the Creator; it now refers to Self. This system contains interlocked and enormously powerful drives toward both Creation and destruction. The creative drive provides humankind with many useful goods and services; the destructive drive depletes nature's resources. Socialist systems for the most part have emulated the developed leading capitalist countries and their environmental impacts are hardly distinguishable from those in other situations.

Is it possible for the economic system to curb its destructive drive and transform its creative drive into a benign environmental force? There is absolutely nothing in the historic record to encourage such a belief. The purpose of our economy has always been to maximize profits, never to serve social ends. Mainstream economic theory since Adam Smith has insisted that by *directly* maximizing profit the entrepreneur is *indirectly* serving the community. All the capital owners together, maximizing their individual profits, produce what the community needs while keeping each other in check by their mutual competition. All this is true but what is also true is the fact that in their single-minded pursuit of profit, in which none can refuse to join on pain of elimination, they are driven to accumulate even more capital, and this becomes both their subjective goal and a motor force of the entire economic system.

A system driven by capital accumulation is one that never stands still, one that is forever changing, adopting new and discarding old methods of production and distribution, opening up new territories, subjecting to its purposes societies too weak to protect themselves. Caught up in this restless innovation and expansion, the system rides roughshod over even its own beneficiaries if they get in its way or fall by the roadside. As far as the natural environment is concerned, our economy perceives it not as something to be cherished and enjoyed but as a means to profit-making and still more capital accumulation.

Such is the inner nature, of the economic system that has generated the present environmental crisis. Naturally it does not operate without opposition. Conservation movements in this century have succeeded in imposing certain limits on the more destructive depredations of uncontrolled use of nature as "raw" resource.

Without such constraints, our economy by now would have destroyed both its environment and itself. Such constraints, however, never go so far as to threaten the economic system as a whole. The system makes some adjustments but not enough to resolve the environmental crisis and the crisis continues to deepen. There is nothing in the record or on the horizon that could lead us to believe the situation will change in the foreseeable future. If this conclusion is accepted, the only alternative to solve the environmental crisis and to ensure that humanity has a future, is to implement an economy to meet real human needs and to restore and sustain nature to a healthy condition.

Lest one should come to a quick answer to our problems by pointing a blaming finger at the United States, the West, or capitalism, it is pertinent to observe that the socialist economies are in a state of deep crisis as well. They show no signs of having found a way out, their near-term outlook is bleak and the longer-term prospects are hard to predict.

In the area of ecology and environment, the record of socialist economies is as dismal, if not worse than that of the capitalist economies. Eastern Europe's air, water and soil are being polluted at an alarming rate although in recent times an environmental awakening has begun. The Polish Academy of Science said a third of the nation's 38 million people live in "areas of ecological disaster." It said conditions were most hazardous in the coal and steel belt of Cracow and Silesia. A Czechoslovak minister told reporters that the life expectancy in his country fell between five and seven years below rates in Western Europe and that it is as much as 11 years shorter in heavily industrialized northwest Bohemia (*New York Times*, June 17,1990).

While the environmental situation seems rather bad right now, if the socialist countries continue to use the central planning process, and are willing to adapt their planning system to serving the needs of the day, they have a good chance of effectively addressing environmental issues. The Western economy with its eye on the short-run gains and a dislike for long-range planning, does not seem to have that inherent possibility.

Can Free Markets Control Pollution?

Over the last 20 years, the managers of American industry have gradually become accustomed to the demands of environmental regulation. The chief requirement up until now has been the installation, wherever possible, of control devices that trap or destroy pollutants that would otherwise enter the environment: the catalytic converters attached to vehicle exhaust systems to remove carbon monoxide, or the scrubbers installed in power plants to trap sulfur dioxide. The Environmental Protection Agency (EPA) has relied on such devices to achieve the reduction in pollution mandated by law.

It is now evident that this "command and control" strategy has failed. For example, the EPA expected the prescribed automobile exhaust controls to reduce annual carbon monoxide emissions by 80 percent and nitrogen oxides by 70 percent between 1975 and 1985. But in that period carbon monoxide emissions fell only 19 percent and nitrogen oxides increased 4 percent. The trends in other standard air pollutants are similar.

Yet, annual emissions of lead into the air have fallen 94 percent since 1975, suggesting that there are right and wrong ways of reducing pollution. The very few successes—lead, DDT, PCB's, strontium 90 are examples—that tell us what works. In each case, substantial improvement was achieved not by tacking a control device onto the process that generates the pollutant, but by *eliminating the pollutant from the production process itself.*

Pollution prevention calls for replacing the production technologies that now assault the environment with processes that are inherently free of pollutants. Such technologies, which are both ecologically and—in the long run—economically sound, exist. If farmers would shift to sustainable organic agriculture, the rising tide of agricultural chemicals that now pollute water supplies would be reversed, and food would be freed of pesticide-derived carcinogens. If automobiles were powered by stratified-charge engines, which sharply reduce nitrogen oxide emissions, the urban pall of smog and ozone would be lifted. If brewers and soft drink industry were forbidden to put plastic nooses on six-packs; if McDonalds rediscovered the paper plate; if the use of plastics was limited to those products for which they are essential, we could push back the petrochemical industry's toxic invasion of the environment.

There is something fundamentally wrong with our economic thinking today. Many economists seem to think that the economy is a flow in a single direction between two infinities: infinite resources on one side, and on the other side an infinite hole into which we can dump all our wastes. They are generally aware that petroleum and other raw materials will eventually disappear, but they believe in a never-ending succession of substitutions such as fission and fusion power, a solar based hydrogen economy and so on.

However, nature does not work that way. Life continues to exist because life was never based on the consumption of resources but on the perfect recycling of resources. In living systems everything is eternally recycled: the flows are circular and closed, not linear and open. In nature's provision for death and decay, true life is sustained. In our economy's provision for permanence and non-destructibility, death is assured. The Scriptural admonition is *choose* life—*true* life. Such life comes through death and resurrection!

We tend to forget that economics is merely a chapter in the story of ecology. Economics deals with the interactions and flow of resources between humans. Ecology deals with life as a whole, of which we humans are only a part. So, true economics must be based on good ecology. It must be based on a different world view.

For Reflection & Group Discussion

1. What would an economy based on stability rather than on growth look like? Brainstorm.

2. Do some household "ecological accounting." Choose an item from your refrigerator, garage or closet. Drawing on your knowledge from previous chapters, list as many costs involved in its production as you can think of. Include hidden ones which have probably been transferred to third parties or the future.

3. Do you believe it is possible for capitalism to create an ecologically sound system?

PART VI

The Human Future

13
WHAT ABOUT
THE FUTURE?

Some of the chapters of this book paint a gloomy picture of the present and the future. Humanity and other species are clearly at risk from industrial society's pollution of the biosphere. Who cares about the future of "nature" or even future generations? For most of us these are not compelling concepts.

In his revised book, *An Inquiry Into the Human Prospect*, Robert L. Heilbroner includes a postscript, entitled "What Has Posterity Ever Done For Me?." He says:

> *"Will mankind survive? Who knows? The question I want to put is more searching: who cares? It is clear that most of us today do not care—or at least do not care enough. How many of us would be willing to give up some minor inconvenience—say, the use of aerosols—in the hope that this might extend the life of man on earth by a hundred years? Suppose we also knew with a high degree of certainty that humankind could not survive a thousand years unless we gave up our wasteful diet of meat, abandoned pleasure driving, cut back on every use of energy that was not essential to the maintenance of a bare minimum. Would we care enough for posterity to pay the price of its survival?"*

Heilbroner doubts that we would care enough. Yet, his willingness to connect the growth economy and the physical limits of the ecosphere is rare among economists. Why so? Because respected economists have asked, "What is so desirable about an indefinite continuation of the human species, religious convictions apart?" For them, we as the human species do not matter because humans are such a minor fraction in time in the billions of years of the earth's history. Moreover, in the 1980 revision of his *Inquiry*, Heilbroner projected a continuing (but gradually slowing) growth economy until the middle of the first decade of the next century. When that ends, he sees the need for highly authoritarian governments to control the transition to economic decline.

Is it too late for a turn around? Does the human race have the humility to confess its addictions, in repentance ask for forgiveness, and then face the future with courage, conviction, and the determination to make things happen? These questions have no simple answers. Whatever the answers, it is obvious to most thinking persons that radical changes in social policies and personal behavior will be required to stem environmental degradation. Without such changes the earth's ability to sustain life will be damaged beyond repair. We may fail to change in time or we may, in desperation, intensify both our exploitation of the earth and our oppression of one another until environmental life-support systems collapse beneath human abuse. Yet the human civilization does possess skills which can assure good and satisfying lives for most people. Life in communion with God, in harmony with nature, and in fellowship with one another is still possible upon the earth. If we really believe this, what needs to the be done?

The preceding chapters of the book, suggest changes in outlook that may be necessary in order to confront environmental problems. For example, in the chapter on nature we have introduced the concept of nature's rights. Or in the section on rain forests, the obvious approach to a solution is to find sustainable ways to stop the destruction while providing for the needs of those who would be affected by those decisions. Many changes will have to be made. However, here we will direct our attention to changes related to our theology, lifestyles and economics.

Theology

What is wrong here? Why doesn't our theology give direction such that we would have avoided this utilitarian view of nature to begin with? Three responses are suggested:

First, it is because we have denied God as Creator—not in word, but in deed. Our once rich theology which was one of

Creation, Fall, Redemption, and living the Christian life has been diminished. Perhaps, because of our utilitarian economic system—our self-centered worldview—we have reshaped our theology to be restricted to salvation history and personal fulfillment. Whatever its cause, our theology has raised little concern for the degradation and dismantling of Creation. Our theology has been silent on Creation's destruction. Earth-keepers have become *practically* (i.e., in practice) meaningless.

Second, as we begin to attempt to understand the meaning and purpose of the world of nature in the overall plan of God's Creation and redemption, we find that theology has largely restricted its attention on the political/historical and the psychological. The cosmological context has been virtually ignored for the past two hundred years. Nature has been dropped from the agenda of theology.

Third, denying God as Creator (in our deeds) ultimately weakens our theology of salvation and inner life, since these depend upon remembering God as Creator. And, being indifferent to the whole of God's Creation represents a distortion of our biblical roots and an insensitivity to the presence of the Holy Spirit in our age. Both for the sake of our faith and for the survival of the environment we have to make radical changes in our understanding of what it means to be a Christian in relation to the rest of the Creation. Any counsel that suggests that Christians can simply ignore the desecration of the Earth believing it will be destroyed anyway or that God only saves people's souls, flatly denies the truth of the Bible. Giving up the environment to the powers of destruction denies that the Earth is the Lord's and is in plain disobedience to the teaching of the biblical tradition that underlies the Christian faith.

A recognition that God loves this Creation should impel us to treat it with respect. We could expand the scriptural model of a steward and apply it to the whole relationship between humanity and the rest of Creation. If we understand humans as being *part* of that Creation, then we can learn how to live with it in humility and mutual interdependence. Living with the rest of Creation includes learning to live with the rest of humanity in a just and equitable way.

We are all bound together, connected in one whole of which the risen Christ is the heart and soul. In Genesis 1, we read that God made humanity in divine image mirroring God's care and sustaining love for God's creatures, to exercise dominion over

Creation, that is, to nurture and care for Creation as God does for us. All is made in Christ and all is redeemed in Christ. We are not an aggregate of individuals, but a community of life.

Any ethics (the science of applying theology in the human context) needs to begin with our interconnectedness within Creation. We can call this ecology but perhaps the term "stewardship" is more helpful. All Creation is God's household. In the past we have been too anthropocentric, but we do have a particular role as human beings. Now we are called to live with other created beings as a household together. We are stewards of a community. We are called to care for the whole household of God, to live in a way which respects our integrity as humans, and nurtures the whole household (Luke 16:1-13; 1 Cor. 4:1, 9:17; Eph. 1:10, 4:29; 1 Pet. 4:10). We are beginning to understand something about ecology, the prudence of living together in a world of limited resources. We have barely begun to explore stewardship, the art of nurturing all Creation as made and redeemed in Christ, with its own proper share in a common future in God.

What might this mean for our approach to agriculture, acid rain, armaments? What difference does it make that as we interact with non-human Creation we are helping to shape its eternal future as well as ours?

In our exploration of the biblical concept of covenant, we discovered that God has made the most generous covenant—to create, liberate and sustain humanity as an integral part of all Creation. Our response to God's love is choosing to care for all life and the whole Creation. We can do no less than to protect and nurture the Earth and all that dwells therein. Making thoughtful, deliberate changes in our theology can be a spiritually uplifting experience for us.

The World Council of Churches (WCC) has provided valuable leadership since the 1983 WCC Assembly in Vancouver on the theme Justice, Peace, and the Integrity of Creation (JPIC). The integrity of Creation is a new element that is exciting and very timely for the attention of the member churches.

The WCC has sponsored gatherings of theologians, church representatives and environmentalists to help articulate new ways of understanding our relationship to God's Creation and what we must do to protect the Earth. It has developed a process that should lead to churches around the world covenanting with each other to work together to protect the environment. It has produced useful worship and discussion materials (see Appendix E).

In March 1990, about 800 persons from around the world met in Korea for the World Council of Churches' Convocation on JPIC. Materials related to this convocation provide additional resources for churches to work for the preservation of Creation (see Appendix E).

The Issue of Lifestyles

Early on we observed that to survive on earth, human beings require the stable, continuing existence of a suitable environment. Yet the evidence is overwhelming that the way in which we now live on the earth is driving its thin, life-supporting skin, and ourselves with it, to destruction. We have a kind of ambiguity in our relation to the environment. Biologically, humans *participate* in the environmental system as parts of the whole. Yet human society is designed to *exploit* the environment as a whole, to produce wealth. The paradoxical role we play in the natural environment—at once participant and exploiter—distorts our perception of it just as it has distorted our theology. As a result we find ourselves in serious trouble with the problems compounding with every passing year. We have arrived at a point in time where environmental threats vie with nuclear war as a preeminent peril to our species.

What shall we do? Will changes in individual lifestyle make a difference? Would recycling, saving energy, planting trees, population control do it? Is simple life the answer? Should we all become vegetarians? We can add many more questions to this list but while all of these are important in themselves, they do not provide all the answers to resolve our predicament. For those who wish to know more about what they can do personally, we have provided in Appendix B, a list of organizations and action-oriented guides and resources which should prove helpful.It is important for each one of us to take whatever steps we can without waiting for others to come along, while at the same time planning for ways to involve others in a joint effort.

The issue is much larger than what appears on the surface. Experts in ecology are increasingly convinced that the survival of the human race, perhaps of all life on the planet, hangs in the balance. If we do not immediately and decisively alter our entire relationship to nature, there is good reason to believe that within

20 years we will have done irrevocable damage to the life-support systems of the planet.

Economics

We could all make environmentally more conscious decisions in our personal lives—recycle, drive less, and so on. But the real and pressing danger to the planet comes from the corporations and governments that decide to use resources and develop products in environmentally destructive and irresponsible ways. By focusing attention on the smaller issues in our personal lives, we get to feel good about ourselves and close our eyes to the larger structural issues which we sometimes feel powerless to change.

Common arguments such as, "people's attitudes have to be changed," or that "if people did not buy environmentally destructive products, corporations would not make them," and so on, have some validity but they do not go far enough. The argument misses the economic and political realities that help shape our choices, and hence unfairly blames the people for choices that are at least understandable given the options they face.

Take, for example, one of heaviest polluters—the automobile. The immense power of the auto and oil industries around the world has been mobilized to block the development of a rational system of mass transportation. In Los Angeles, for example, a rail transit system was bought up and dismantled by an automobile manufacturer—so that people would become more dependent on cars. Other powerful corporations, using their resources to encourage the election of sympathetic legislators, managed to prevent the introduction of serious auto-emission restraints, thus polluting major industrial areas. In such circumstances, the choice to live in suburbia and drive to work makes a lot of sense. To blame the individual consumers for making this choice or to ask them to raise their environmental consciousness misses the point.

Similarly the Third World has become a ready target for global environmental ills, e.g., those who cut down the rain forests. Here again, the real issue is the larger economic realities that have caused the problem in the first place. For hundreds of years Western colonialists, and for decades American corporate interests have helped shape a world economy that has prevented Third World countries from developing economic independence. Economic arrangements imposed on the Third World by the technologically powerful developed world have often caused massive poverty for their people. The net outcome of this process is larger profits for corporations and their publics from cheap raw materials, cheap labor, and markets for goods. For most Third World peoples, physical survival comes before pious environmental platitudes and sermons from Western environmentalists.

Corporations will take a few minimal steps to project an image of corporate sensitivity to environmental issues but they will not change their behavior as long as it is profitable for them to produce goods that may have long-term destructive consequences. After all, they are in the business of maximizing profits in the short-run for their shareholders. Minimal steps for good public relations are fine, but corporations certainly are not going to engage in a fundamental restructuring of what and how to produce.

It is as wrong to point fingers at corporate managers as it is to attack individual workers in environmentally destructive ventures. All are caught in a web of entanglements in which it will be self-destructive to their own short-term interests to act in ways that would be environmentally rational.

Without some big changes, Planet Earth is doomed. Perhaps we need an international system for rational planning of industrial production, farming, fishing, mining, energy resources, and the like. The human race *could* pull together, decide to prohibit all forms of interference with the natural environment that are destructive to the long-term survival of the human race, and enforce its decisions. But that cannot happen without a moral revolution. After all, most of our problems are beyond technological solutions. The crisis is one of moral and ethical choices that can keep and tend God's good Creation.

Eco-Justice

Eco-Justice is a relatively new word. It symbolizes the conviction that issues of justice and ecology are of crucial importance and that human survival depends upon dealing with both. Eco-Justice offers a different way of looking at the world.

Eco-Justice provides us a way of looking at economic issues through the lens of environmental health, and looking at environmental issues through the lens of economic justice. The word eco-justice emphasizes that the "economic" and the "ecological" are not two separate categories but rather two facets of the *same* issue, which is, the sustainable well-being of all of Creation. It promotes the protection of a healthy environment and justice for all people.

The economic and the ecological are the flip sides of the same concern for the earth and its creatures. William A. Gibson writes, "Theologies of Creation must not neglect the liberation of people. Creation includes humanity. Nature and the poor are both victims of oppression. They will be liberated together or not at all. The term eco-justice ... is not turning away from concern for justice in the social order but ... combining justice for people with justice to the rest of Creation."

For the Presbyterian Eco-Justice Task Force, eco-justice adds a major insight—that justice to human beings is inseparable from right relationships with and within the natural order. Eco-Justice for the Task Force also means justice to all of God's Creation. This can be a daunting task.

A number of community organizations have undertaken the daunting task of eco-justice (for a partial listing, see Appendix C). They portray the real story of people living out the Gospel doing eco-justice. A number of stories could be told about these modern "saints" some of whom gave higher priority to active involvement in the caring of Creation, instead of singing in the choir, for example.

Should churches and congregations be involved in eco-justice activities? What are the models for such involvement? One possible model is obvious in the true story of what took place in Woburn, Massachusetts—an unknown town, now known nationwide—with one of the 10 most hazardous waste sites in the United States. Lagoons of toxic arsenic, lead, and chromium cover a tract of 300 acres representing poisonous wastes, left behind by chemical manufacturers and tanneries no longer operating in the area.

The story centers around a small boy named Jimmy Anderson, who died at the age of 12 after nearly a lifelong battle with acute lymphocratic leukemia. Anne Anderson, Jimmy's mother was determined to ferret out the cause of her son's illness amid inconclusive fragments of data. Her search confirmed her worst suspicions. Her son had been poisoned, in his own home, simply by drinking the water that came out of the tap. Moreover, she was sure that Jimmy's illness, along with the leukemia of twelve children in East Woburn, was caused by industrial contaminants. Six children lived within a ten-minute walk of her home.

A number of actors—the medical experts, the citizens of Woburn, the senators and other public officials, the various governmental agencies and departments—were involved in the story. But for our purposes, the central figure is an affable and unassuming Episcopal priest, the Reverend Bruce Young, rector of Trinity Church in Woburn. Through his ministry to the Anderson family and to another parishioner, Donna Robbins, and her son, who developed leukemia and later died, he became involved in issues that reach far beyond his parish and his own town. These issues have enormous financial, legal, and medical implications for the interrelationships of corporations, governments, and young boys like Jimmy.

Reverend Bruce Young was called to be rector of Woburn's Trinity Church in 1966. He did not come to Woburn with a particular expectation of social activism but he wasn't a complete novice at it either. An important part—18 years out of 24—of his ministry in Woburn has been around the issue of environmental pollution and the involvement with the problem of toxic waste evolved out of his pastoral concern. Initially, at her husband's request Bruce tried to talk Anne Anderson out of her notion that water had caused her son's illness. But in 1979 when they prepared a map and saw how many cases of leukemia were in a small area, he became a believer in Anne's suspicions about the water and pursued it to get someone with expertise to look at the issue.

Bruce Young called a public meeting in 1979 at the Trinity Church. The national attention to the cluster mystery in Woburn resulted from the efforts of many—starting with Young and the community Group FACE (For A Cleaner Environment), the organization he and Anne Anderson were instrumental in founding. FACE continued its mission at the state and federal levels including Senator Edward M. Kennedy's involvement in 1980 in drafting the Comprehensive Environmental Response Compensation and Liability Act—Superfund. He asked Bruce Young and Anne Anderson to testify at Senate hearings, which they did.

These past years have not been easy for Bruce Young. Enlightened self interest might direct anyone in his position not to become involved in the sad events of his city. The publicity given to Woburn has made some of the townspeople uncomfortable, even angry. Some fear that real estate values may be adversely affected.

Bruce Young's congregation at Trinity is not of one mind on his involvement in the issue. Not everyone in his parish has enthusiastically applauded his efforts. Many parishioners are glad that (largely through the rector) Trinity has been a part of this ministry.

In the midst of this tragic story, Bruce Young has found the possibilities of redemption. "My motivation now is being able to have Woburn stand as the place where all this pain and agony, the publicity and television cameras, the engineer's salaries, all of what has happened here, has produced something: a new understanding of the cause of leukemia, which won't only make a difference here, but in Italy and Idaho and everywhere there is toxic waste."

He believes that one of the best things that could come out of all of this would be increased awareness of the problem, so that the Woburn story is not repeated.

The Woburn story is not yet ended. The story has been the subject of one book (see Appendix B), national television coverage, and has been the subject of numerous magazine and newspaper articles. Perhaps it will alert other companies to proper handling of toxic wastes as even more than a legal necessity. Perhaps there will be widespread changes in corporate policies and practices concerning use and disposal of hazardous substances. Perhaps, citizens of other towns will be awakened to possible environmental hazards. Perhaps as citizens of Planet Earth, we will come to a more vigorous safeguarding of "this fragile earth, our island home."

With thousands of toxic waste sites located across the United States, and the many ways we have polluted the Earth, there may be numerous stories like Jimmy Anderson's that we have not heard about or are likely to hear about. The Church teaches us to "choose life," and if that is its teaching, is it appropriate for churches to get involved in "Creation-related" issues which, by the nature of the culture we live in, are political?

A Challenge and a Call to the Churches

The real challenge to the churches on eco-justice issues comes from outside—not from the feeble few within the body of believers who are concerned and care enough to work on them. The challenge is from the Creation to the Church. Ask the

Creation to "stop groaning" and find out what emotions it provokes in you. Stand next to a garbage dump site and say to the Creation "stop groaning." In all honesty, you just cannot say that to Creation. Creation is speaking loudly and we must respond.

The magnitude of social, economic and political changes that will be necessary to achieve a vision for justice to all of God's Creation, can be overwhelming. All industrialized societies have built themselves on two erroneous beliefs: that the natural resources necessary for material well-being are infinite and that the biosphere (air, land and water) is capable of endlessly absorbing poisonous wastes. Simply to recognize the wrongheadedness of these two assumptions and to adapt our actions to ecological reality will be a herculean task. For that task will involve revolutionary changes in industrial and agricultural methods, cessation of some kinds of production, and a lifestyle of curtailed consumption for some. The *Global 2000 Report to President Carter* attempted to make this point, but most people were paralysed at the prospect and still refuse to face ecological reality, vainly hoping that it will go away.

Undergirding our present mind-set are familiar sins of pride and idolatry. Moreover, Western Christianity has a strong hierarchical tradition which has fostered domination over people and nature. This "antiegalitarian, patriarchal, and nature-dominating theology" set up hierarchy with God at the top, followed by men, women, children, animals and plants—in that order. We used or accepted the use of Scripture to justify arrogance, or remained silent when political theorists asserted the sanctity of human freedom to exploit resources. The Christian tradition chose to understand Genesis 1:28 as a divine commandment to conquer every part of nature and make it humankind's slave. Certainly such an interpretation proved useful over the centuries as intellectual lubrication for the exploitation of nature. Indeed, was this not one of the main reasons for its initial appearance and persistence in Christian thought?

We have relied on our own wits to solve the problems arising from acting on such misconception of reality, counting on the next "techno-fix" to rescue us from our own folly. And we have put our trust in an ever growing supply of material resources to avoid the hard, self-sacrificial, sharing that the contemporary situation requires of us.

The struggle to accept our own fallibility and the interconnectedness of all Creation is daunting. But it is almost dwarfed by the dilemmas which accompany a sounder vision: how to heal a poisoned planet while ensuring just distribution of the costs and benefits of doing so? This translates most obviously into questions of employment, investment of capital, and "cost." "Cost" must be redefined to include loss of jobs, community disruption, and effects of pollution on people and ecosystems. We must develop methods that allow citizens who will be affected by a given action to be involved in policy decision-making.

Overall, the churches have shown lively concern for economic justice issues. Many local church and community leaders insist that the immediate needs of persons for jobs and economic security must take precedence over all other issues. In the midst of such a situation, it is counterproductive to pose these two issues—ecological wholeness and economic justice—against each other. We need to find creative patterns and new ways of looking at the world.

In a recent conference David Brower, a prominent environmentalist appealed to the churches to become involved in earth healing. He said, "Environmental problems are as serious as anything that we have to confront on this earth. Anyone who is observing what is going on outdoors can see what is happening to the air, the water, the soil, and what we are doing with our technology, our overconsumption, our thoughtlessness about the future of the earth. We cannot have peace on earth unless we make peace with the earth. This is going to ... particularly require the best organized sector of human society, the Church."

There is no question that the key to the environmental crisis is the power inherent in the churches. They have the potential to fire the conscience of their membership into renewed activity on behalf of the Earth. Some churches are doing well with organizing their membership for continued action for restoring Creation. For example, more than half of the Annual Conferences of the United Methodist Church in the United States have active committees on environmental justice. The Women's Division of the United Methodist Church in the U.S., has made eco-justice a four year priority for study and action to save the environment. Every church needs to give priority attention to caring for God's Creation.

A second area where the churches are called to act is in making serious efforts to interpret the historical "sin-and-salvation" focus in light of the ecological crisis and to rediscover the meaning of "sin." Some of this has been discussed above under the section on theology. Up until now science had no room for God and theology has excluded science. God was outside the universe except for occasional interventions in the form of miracles. But there was always the reservation that God was more intimately involved in human life, though not in the rest of nature. The 1979 World Council of Churches Conference on Faith, Science and Technology concluded that this is still the dominant position today in the Western world. It has been disastrous for science and theology and nature.

A third area for the churches to work on is in their need to understand that the world is no longer a factory for the exclusive use of human beings. It is alive with God. It is not only human beings who are of value. Whenever there is life and feeling there is intrinsic value. God values the whole of nature. The non-human Creation is not simply the stage on which the drama of human life is performed. It is itself part of the drama with all creatures in their varying degrees participating in the joys and suffering of Creation. If that be true, it is crucial that we respect the non-human Creation. It is crucial that we move away from our anthropocentric ethic to a life-centered ethic.

We are called to fight oppression wherever it exists both in human life and in non-human life. We are called upon to look after nature, not only because nature looks after us but also because nature has its own intrinsic value to itself and to God. If the churches have any concern at all about saving the integrity of nature, they will need to come into the picture with a specific Christian understanding of the relation of nature, humanity and God.

A fourth area for churches to consider is what has been described as making every church a Creation Awareness Center. Churches that seek to view the environmental problem biblically and theologically are bound to conclude that the mission of the church today brings Christians into engagement with God in keeping and healing the Creation.

To make a church a Creation Awareness Center could involve undertaking a variety of activities for children, youth, adults, the building committee, the hunger task force of the church and so on. The idea is to undertake an assessment of the church's current involvement in earthkeeping, to make celebrating God's ongoing Creation a priority and to make eco-justice an important part of the church's ministry.

The environment does not depend upon humans. It is clearly the other way around. The question is whether we humans are willing to acknowledge the seriousness of our situation and to work diligently to turn things around or whether we would do nothing because many of the damaging results of the degradations are not readily visible to the naked eye. Our success or failure will depend upon a great many small decisions and actions as well as some large decisions but the carrying out will be in terms of specific, discrete decisions and actions.

As Christians, we can reform our theology and contribute to society a new appreciation for the sacredness of all Creation. Individually and collectively, we can change the way we live so that instead of destroying the earth, we can help it to thrive, today and for future generations. The Creator-Redeemer seeks the renewal of the Creation and calls the people of God to participate in saving acts of renewal. We are called to cooperate with God in transforming a world that has not fulfilled its divinely given potential. Our task is to join God in preserving, renewing and fulfilling the Creation. It is to relate to nature in ways that ensure life on Planet Earth, provide for the basic needs of all humankind, and increase justice and well-being for all life in a peaceful world.

For Reflection and Group Discussion

1. What *has* posterity ever done for you? What (or whom) do you think about when you imagine the world a hundred years from now?

2. Do you agree that theology must change with the times? If so, what changes need to be made in light of the fragile condition of the earth today?

3. "Any ethics needs to begin with our interconnectedness." What might this mean for your approach to the ecological concern your group is most eager to work on?

4. How important are personal lifestyle changes in the face of the ecological crisis? How do you respond to the statement that by "focusing attention on the smaller issues in

our personal lives, we get to feel good about ourselves and close our eyes to the larger structural issues..."?

5. This chapter suggests that consumers are often victimized by larger structures. It also says that corporate managers are themselves caught in a web of entanglements and unable to act appropriately. Who exactly *is* to blame? How would you define sin and evil in light of the ecological crisis?

6. "Nature and the poor are both victims of oppression. They will be liberated together or not at all." What examples can you give to support this statement? Do the two goals ever seem at odds?

7. The word "humility" is used several times in this chapter. What is your definition of humility? How might it help heal the ecological crisis?

8. Review the four calls to churches listed in the last section of this chapter. Adopt, revise or rewrite them for your own setting.

9. Commemorate this study and your care for Creation with a banner. Try one of the following sentences as a take off point:

"We are all bound together, connected in one whole of which the risen Christ is the heart and soul." (p.121)

"We cannot have peace on earth unless we make peace with the earth." (p.130)

APPENDIX A

THE WORLD CHARTER FOR NATURE
(Adopted by United Nations General Assembly on October 26, 1982)

The General Assembly

Reaffirming the fundamental purposes of the United Nations, in particular maintenance of international peace and security, the development of friendly relations among nations and the achievement of International co-operation in solving international problems of an economic, social, cultural, technical, intellectual or humanitarian character,

Aware that:

a) Mankind is a part of nature and life depends on the uninterrupted functioning of natural systems which ensure the supply of energy and nutrients,

b) Civilization is rooted in nature, which has shaped human culture and influenced all artistic and scientific achievement, and living in harmony with nature gives man the best opportunities for the development of his creativity, and for rest and recreation,

Convinced that:

a) Every form of life is unique, warranting respect regardless of its worth to man, and, to accord other organisms such recognition, man must be guided by a moral code of action,

b) Man can alter nature and exhaust natural resources by his action or its consequences and, therefore, must fully recognize the urgency of maintaining the stability and quality of nature and of conserving natural resources,

Persuaded that:

a) Lasting benefits from nature depend upon the maintenance of essential ecological processes and life support systems, and upon the diversity of life forms, which are jeopardized through excessive exploitation and habitat destruction by man,

b) The degradation of natural systems owing to excessive consumption and misuse of natural resources, as well as to failure to establish an appropriate economic order among peoples and among states, leads to the breakdown of the economic, social and political framework of civilization,

c) Competition for scarce resources creates conflicts, whereas the conservation of nature and natural resources contributes to justice and the maintenance of peace and cannot be achieved until mankind learns to live in peace and to forsake war and armaments,

Reaffirming that man must acquire the knowledge to maintain and enhance his ability to use natural resources in a manner which ensures the preservation of the species and ecosystems for the benefit of present and future generations,

Firmly convinced of the need for appropriate measures, at the national and international, individual and collective, and private and public levels, to protect nature and promote international co-operating in this field,

Adopts, to these ends, the present World Charter for Nature, which proclaims the following principles of conversation by which all human conduct affecting nature is to be guided and judged.

I. General Principles

1. Nature shall be respected and its essential processes shall not be impaired.

2. The genetic viability on the earth shall not be compromised; the population levels of all life forms, wild and domesticated, must be at least sufficient for their survival, and to this end necessary habitats shall be safeguarded.

3. All areas of the earth, both land and sea, shall be subject to these principles of conservation; special protection shall be given to unique areas, to representative samples of all the different types of ecosystems and to the habitats of rare or endangered species.

4. Ecosystems and organisms, as well as the land, marine and atmospheric resources that are utilized by man, shall be managed to achieve and maintain optimum sustainable productivity, but not in such a way as to endanger the integrity of those other ecosystems or species with which they coexist.

5. Nature shall be secured against degradation caused by warfare or other hostile activities.

II. Functions

6. In the decisionmaking process it shall be recognized that man's needs can be met only by ensuring the proper functioning of natural systems and by respecting the principles set forth in the present Charter.

7. In the planning and implementation of social and economic development activities, due account shall be taken of the fact that the conservation of nature is an integral part of those activities.

8. In formulating long-term plans for economic development, population growth and the improvement of standards of living, due account shall be taken of the long-term capacity of natural systems to ensure the subsistence and settlement of the populations concerned, recognizing that this capacity may be enhanced through science and technology.

9. The allocation of areas of the earth to various uses shall be planned, and due account shall be taken of the physical constraints, the biological productivity and diversity and the natural beauty of the areas concerned.

10. Natural resources shall not be wasted, but used with a restraint appropriate to the principles set forth in the present Charter, in accordance with the following rules:

    a) Living resources shall not be utilized in excess of their natural capacity for regeneration;

    b) The productivity of soils shall be maintained or enhanced through measures which safeguard their long-term fertility and the process of organic decomposition, and prevent erosion and all other forms of degradation;

    c) Resources, including water, which are not consumed as they are used shall be reused or recycled;

    d) Non-renewable resources which are consumed as they are used shall be exploited with restraint, taking into account their abundance, the rational possibilities of converting them for consumption, and the compatibility of their exploitation with the functioning of natural systems.

11. Activities which might have an impact on nature shall be controlled, and the best available technologies that minimize significant risks to nature or other adverse effects shall be used; in particular;

    a) Activities which are likely to cause irreversible damage to nature shall be avoided;

    b) Activities which are likely to pose a significant risk to nature shall be preceded by an exhaustive examination; their proponents shall demonstrate that expected benefits outweigh potential damage to nature, and where potential adverse effects are not fully understood, the activities should not proceed;

    c) Activities which may disturb nature shall be preceded by assessment of their consequences, and environmental impact studies of development projects shall be conducted sufficiently in advance, and if they are to be undertaken, such activities shall be planned and carried out so as to minimize potential adverse effects;

    d) Agriculture, grazing, forestry and fisheries practices shall be adapted to the natural characteristics and constraints of given areas;

    e) Areas degraded by human activities shall be rehabilitated for purposes in accord with their natural potential and compatible with the well-being of affected populations.

12. Discharge of pollutants into natural systems shall be avoided and:

    a) Where this is not feasible, such pollutants shall be treated at the source, using the best practicable means available;

    b) special precautions shall be taken to prevent discharge of radioactive or toxic wastes.

13. Measures intended to prevent, control or limit natural disasters, infestations and diseases shall be specifically directed to the causes of these scourges and shall avoid adverse side-effects on nature.

III. Implementation

14. The principles set forth in the present Charter shall be reflected in the law and practice of each State, as well as at the international level.

15. Knowledge of nature shall be broadly disseminated by all possible means, particularly by ecological education as an integral part of general education.

16. All planning shall include, among its essential elements, the formulation of strategies for the conservation of nature, the establishment of inventories of ecosystems and assessments of the effects on nature of proposed policies and activities; all of these elements shall be disclosed to the public by appropriate means in time to permit effective consultation and participation.

17. Funds, programmes and administrative structures necessary to achieve the objective of the conservation of nature shall be provided.

18. Constant efforts shall be made to increase knowledge of nature by scientific research and to disseminate such knowledge unimpeded by restrictions of any kind.

19. The status of natural processes, ecosystems and species shall be closely monitored to enable early detection of degradation or threat, ensure timely intervention and facilitate the evaluation of conservation policies and methods.

20. Military activities damaging to nature shall be avoided.

21. States and, to the extent they are able, other public authorities, international organizations, individuals, groups and corporations shall:

    a) Co-operate in the task of conserving nature through common activities and other relevant actions, including information exchange and consultations;

    b) Establish standards for products and manufacturing processes that may have adverse effects on nature, as well as agreed methodologies for assessing these effects;

    c) Implement the applicable international legal provisions for the conservation of nature and the protection of the environment;

d) Ensure that activities within their jurisdiction or control do not cause damage to the natural systems located within other States or in the areas beyond the limits of national jurisdiction;

e) Safeguard and conserve nature in areas beyond national jurisdiction;

22. Taking fully into account the sovereignty of States over their natural resources, each State shall give effect to the provisions of the present Charter through its competent organs and in co-operation with other States.

23. All persons, in accordance with their national legislation, shall have the opportunity to participate, individually or with others, in the formulation of decisions of direct concern to their environment, and shall have access to means of redress when their environment has suffered damage or degradation.

24. Each person has a duty to act in accordance with the provisions of the present Charter; acting individually, in association with others or through participation in the political process, each person shall strive to ensure that the objectives and requirements of the present Charter are met.

APPENDIX B

FOR FURTHER READING

Nature and Its Rights

Ecology and Religion. John Carmody. New York:Paulist Press, 1983.

Crisis in Eden. Frederick Elder. Nashville and New York:Abingdon Press, 1970.

The Human Presence: An Orthodox View of Nature. Paulos Mar Gregorius. World Council of Churches. 1978.

Wind and Sea Obey Him. Robert Faricy. Westminster, MD:Christian Classics, Inc., 1988.

The Rights of Nature. Roderick Frazier Nash. Madison:The University of Wisconsin Press, 1989.

Ecology and Human Need. Thomas Sieger Derr. Philadelphia:The Westminster Press, 1975.

The End of Nature. Bill McKibben. New York:Random House, 1989.

Planet Earth

Population Explosion. Paul R. Ehrlich and Anne H. Ehrlich. New York:Simon and Schuster, 1990.

Human Ecosystems. W.B. Chapman, Jr. New York:Macmillan Publishing Co., Inc., 1981.

Fundamentals of Ecology. 3rd Edition. Eugene P. Odum. Philadelphia:W. B. Saunders Co., 1971.

Living in the Environment. 3rd Edition. Miller G. Tyler. Belmont, CA:Wadsworth Publishing, 1982.

Ecology of Ancient Civilizations. J. Donald Hughes. Albuquerque:University of New Mexico Press, 1975.

A Protocol for Holy Ground. Marshall Massey. 4353 East 119th Way, Thornton, Co. 80233.

Greenhouse Effect, Ozone

The Greenhouse Effect, Climatic Change, and Ecosystems. Edited by Bert Bolin, B. R. Doos, and Richard A. Warrick. John Wiley & Sons, 1986.

Entropy: Into the Greenhouse World. Jeremy Rifkin. Bantam Revised Edition, 1989.

Global Warming: Are We Entering the Greenhouse Century? Stephen H.
Schneider. Sierra Club Books, 1989.

Altering the Earth's Chemistry: Assessing the Risks. Worldwatch Paper 71,
July 1986; Slowing Global Warming: A Worldwide Strategy.
Worldwatch Paper 91, October 1989.

Protecting the Ozone Layer. Cynthia Pollock Shea. State of the World
Report, 1989, Worldwatch Institute, Washington, D.C.; Protecting
Life on Earth: Steps to Save the Ozone Layer. Worldwatch Paper
87, December 1988.

Magazine Articles: *Newsweek,* July 11, 1988; Time, January 2, 1989;
Scientific American, April 1989, September 1989.

The Greenhouse Gases. UNEP/GEMS Environment Library No.1. UNEP.
New York Liaison Office.

The Ozone Layer. UNEP/GEMS Environment Library No.2. UNEP. New
York Liaison Office.

The Changing Atmosphere. UNEP Environment Brief No.1. State of the
World Report, 1988.

Forests

The Primary Source: Tropical Forests and Our Future. Norman Myers. W.W.
Norton, 1984.

Public Policies and the Misuse of Forest Resources. Roberto Repetto and
Malcolm Gillis. World Resource Institute, 1988.

The Fate of the Forest: Developers, Destroyers and Defenders of the Amazon.
Susanna Hecht and Alexander Cockburn. Verso, 1989.

American Forests: The Magazine of Trees and Forests. Nov/Dec. 1988 issue
on Tropical Deforestation.

In the Rainforest. Catherine Caufield. Chicago:University of Chicago
Press, 1984.

People of the Tropical Rainforest. Julie Sloan Denslow and Christine
Padoch, Eds. University of California Press, 1988.

Bird of Life, Bird of Death: A Political Ornithology of Central America.
Jonathon Evan Maslow. New York:Dell Publishing Co., Inc., 1986.

Water Pollution

Groundwater: A Community Action Guide. By CONCERN, Inc.. 1794
Columbia Road, N.W.. Washington D.C. 20009, 1984.

Ground Water Protection. The Conservation Foundation. 1255 23rd St.
N.W.. Washington, D.C. 20007.

Drinking Water: A Community Action Guide. By CONCERN, Inc., 1986.

State of the World Report, 1985.

Safeguarding the World's Water. United Nations Environment Program.
UNEP Environment Brief No.6.

Economic Poison: Groundwater Quality and Agri-Chemicals. Center for Rural Affairs. P.O.Box 405. Walthill, NE 68067. Special Report. November, 1989.

Cleaning Up the Seas. UNEP Environment Brief No.5.

The Poisoned Well: New Strategies for Groundwater Protection. Sierra Club Legal Defense Fund. Island Press. 1989.

Wastes Accumulation

State of the World Report, 1987, 1988.

Hazardous Chemicals. UNEP Brief No.4.

The Citizens Toxics Protection Manual. published by The National Toxics Campaign. Boston, MA, 1988.

Report to Congress: Solid Waste Disposal in the United States. Environmental Protection Agency. U.S. Government Printing Press, 1989.

The Solid Waste Handbook: A Practical Guide. Edited by William D. Robinson. John Wiley & Sons, Inc., 1986.

Waste: Choices for Communities. Concern, Inc., 1988.

Household Waste: Issues and Opportunities. Concern, Inc., 1989.

Toxic Wastes and Race in the United States: A National Report on the Racial and Socio-Economic Characteristics of Communities With Hazardous Waste Sites. Commission for Racial justice, United Church of Christ, 1987.

Managing Our Wastes, IMPACT Prepare, 1989. Interfaith IMPACT For Justice and Peace, 100 Maryland Ave. NE, Washington, D.C. 20002

Misuse of Land

State of the World Report, 1984.

Sands of Change: Why Land Becomes Desert and What Can Be Done About It. UNEP Brief No. 2.

Farmland: A Community Issue. Concern, Inc., 1987.

Global Dust Bowl: Can We Stop the Destruction of the Land Before It's Too Late? C. Dean Freudenberger. Augsburg, 1990.

Population and Environment

State of the World Reports, 1984, 1987, 1988.

The Population Explosion. Paul R. Ehrlich and Anne H. Ehrlich. Simon and Schuster, 1990.

United Nations Fund for Population Activities. 1990 Annual Report on World Population. United Nations Secretariat. New York City.

Biotechnology and Creation

Altered Harvest : Agriculture, Genetics, and the Fate of the World's Food Supply. Jack Doyle. Viking, 1985.

Biofuture: Confronting the Genetic Era. Burke K. Zimmerman. New York:Plenam Press, 1984.

Biotechnology: The University-Industrial Complex. Martin Kenney. Yale University Press, 1986.

The Gene Business: Who Should Control Biotechnology? Edward Yoxen. Harper and Row, 1983.

Biotechnology: Its Challenges to the Churches and the World; A Report by World Council of Churches Subunit on Church and Society. P.O.Box 2100. 150 route de Ferney. 1211 Geneva 2. Switzerland. August, 1989.

Algeny. Jeremy Rifkin. The Viking Press, 1983.

Human Life and the New Genetics: A Report of a Task Force commissioned by the National Council of the Churches of Christ in the USA, 1980.

Choices for the Heartland: Alternative Directions in Biotechnology and Implications for Family Farming, Rural Communities and the Environment. Chuck Hassebrook and Gabriel Hegyes. Center for Rural Affairs, Walthill, NE 68067.

Ecology, Economy, and Economic Systems

For the Common Good: Redirecting the Economy Toward Community, the Environment, and a Sustainable Future. Herman E. Daly and John B. Cobb, Jr. Boston:Beacon Press, 1989.

God the Economist: The Doctrine of God and Political Economy. M. Douglas Meeks. Minneapolis:Fortress Press, 1989.

The Poverty of Affluence: A Psychological Portrait of the American Way of Life. Paul L. Wachtel. Philadelphia, PA:New Society Publishers, 1989.

Home Economics. Wendell Berry. North Point Press, 1987.

What About the Future

Cluster Mystery: Epidemic and the Children of Woburn, Mass. Paula DiPerna, St. Louis, MO:The C.V. Mosby Company, 1985.

APPENDIX C

SELECTED ENVIRONMENTAL ORGANIZATIONS

Agriculture

Center for Science in the Public Interest, 1501 16th Street, N.W., Washington, D.C. 20036, 202/332-9110.

Institute for Alternative Agriculture, 9200 Edmonston Road, Suite 117, Greenbelt, MD 20770, 301/441-8777.

National Coalition to Stop Food Irradiation, P.O. Box 59-0488, San Francisco, CA 94101, 415/626-2734.

Regenerative Agriculture Association, 222 Main Street, Emmaus, PA 18049, 215/967-5171.

Rodale Research Center, Box 323, RD 1, Kutztown, PA 19530, 215/683-6383.

The Land Institute, 2440 E. Water Well Road, Salina, KS 67401, 913/823-5376.

Seed Saver's Exchange, Rural Route 3, Box 239, Decorah, IA 52101, 319/382-3949.

World Resources Institute, 1709 New York Avenue, N.W., 7th floor, Washington, D.C. 20006, 202/638-6300.

Air Pollution

Concern Inc., 1794 Columbia Road, N.W., Washington, D.C. 20009, 202/328-8160.

National Clean Air Coalition, 530 7th Street, S.W., Washington, D.C. 20003, 202/543-8200.

State and Territorial Air Pollution Program Administration/Air Pollution Control Office (STAPPA and APCO), 444 N. Capitol Street, N.W., Washington, D.C. 20003, 202/674-7864.

Animal Protection

Audubon Society, 950 Third Avenue, New York, NY 10022, 212/832-3200.

Greenpeace, 1436 U Street, S.W., Washington, D.C. 20009, 202/462-1177.

National Coalition for Marine Conservation, P.O. Box 23298, Savannah, GA 31403, 912/234-8062.
National Wildlife Federation, 1412 16th Street, N.W., Washington, D.C. 20036, 202/797-6800.
The Oceanic Society, 1536 16th Street, N.W., Washington, D.C. 20036.
Wilderness Society, 1400 I Street, N.W., Washington, D.C. 20005, 202/842-3400.
World Wildlife Fund/Conservation Foundation, 1250 24th Street, N.W., Washington, D.C. 20037, 202/293-4800.

Energy Conservation

Alliance to Save Energy, 1925 K Street, N.W., Suite 206, Washington, D.C. 20006, 202/857-0666.
American Council for an Energy Efficient Economy, 1001 Connecticut Avenue, N.W. #535, Washington, D.C. 20036.
American Solar Energy Society, 2400 Central Avenue #B1, Boulder, CO 80301, 303/443-3130.
International Institute for Energy Conservation, 420 C Street, N.E., Washington, D.C. 20011, 202/546-3388.
Safe Energy Communication Council, 1717 Massachusetts Avenue, N.W. #11215, Washington, D.C. 20036, 202/483-8491.

Forests

ANAI (Asociacion do los Nuevos Alquimistas), 1176 Bryson City Road, Franklin, NC 28734, (US office of a Costa Rican organization).
Environmental Policy Institute/Friends of the Earth/Oceanic Society, 218 D Street SE, Washington, D. C. 20003, 202/544-2600.
National Resources Defense Council, 1350 New York Ave. NW, Suite 300, Washington, D. C. 20005, 202/783-7800.
National Wildlife Federation, 1412 16th St. NW, Washington, D. C. 20036-2266. 202/797-6800.
Rainforest Action Network, 301 Broadway, San Francisco, CA 94133, 415/398-4404.
Rainforest Alliance, 270 Lafayette St., Suite 512, New York, N.Y. 10012.
Woods Hole Research Center, 13 Church St., P.O. Box 296, Woods Hole, MA 02543, 508/540-9900.
World Wildlife Fund, 1255 23rd St. NW, Suite 200, Washington, D.C. 20037.

Greenhouse Effect

Environmental Defence Fund, 257 Park Ave. S, New York, NY 10010, 212/505-2100.
National Audubon Society, 950 Third Ave., New York, NY 10022, 212/832-3200.

Natural Resources Defence Council, 122 E. 42nd St., New York, NY 10168, 212/727-2700.
National Wildlife Federation, 1400 16th St., NW, Washington, D.C. 20036, 703/790-4321.
Sierra Club, 730 Polk St., San Francisco, CA 94109, 415/776-2211.
Union of Concerned Scientists, 26 Church St., Cambridge, MA 02238, 617/547-5552.
Worldwatch Institute, 1776 Massachusetts Ave., NW, Washington, D.C. 20036, 202/452-1999.
World Resources Institute, 1709 New York Ave., NW, Washington, D.C. 20006, 202/638-6300.
World Wildlife Fund, 1250 24th St., NW, Washington, D.C. 20037, 202/293-4800.
Zero Population Growth, 1400 16th St., NW, Suite 320, Washington, D.C. 20036, 202/332-2200.

Land Conservation

American Forestry Association, Global ReLeaf Program, P.O. Box 2000, Washington, D.C. 20013, (202) 667-3300.
Earth First!, P.O. Box 5871, Tucson, AZ 85703, 602/622-1371.
American Wilderness Alliance, 7600 East Arapahoe, Suite 114, Englewood, CO 80112, 303/771-0380.
National Parks and Conservation 20 Association, 1015 31st Street, N.W., Washington, D.C. 20007, 202/944-8530.
Rainforest Action Network, 300 Broadway, Suite 28, San Francisco, CA 94133, 415/398-4404.
TreePeople, 12601 Mulholland Drive, Beverly Hills, CA 90210, 818/769-2663.

Oceans

Center for Marine Conservation, 1725 DeSales Street,NW, Suite 500, Washington, D.C. 20036. 202/429-5609. An educational organization focused on marine debris and marine mammals.
Chesapeake Bay Foundation, 162 Prince George Street, Annapolis, MD 21401, 301/268-8816. Works to improve the Bay's environment.
Coast Alliance, 1536 16th St. NW, Washington, D.C. 20036, 202/265-5518. Umbrella group for 35 organizations involved in coastal environmental issues.
Council on Ocean Law, 1709 New York Ave. NW, Washington, D.C. 20008, 202/347-3766. Supports the development of international laws for the oceans.
Greenpeace USA, 1426 U Street NW, Washington, D.C. 20036, 202/462-1177. A membership group involved in policy formulation and activism on environmental issues, including oceanic pollution, energy development and fisheries.

International Marinelife Alliance USA, 94 Station Street, Suite 645, Hingham, MA 02043, 617/383-1209. A membership organization that conducts research, education and training to protect marine life worldwide.

OCA/PAC, United Nations Environment Program, P.O.Box 30552, Nairobi, Kenya.

Pesticides and Chemicals

Citizen's Clearinghouse for Hazardous Waste, P.O. Box 926, Arlington, VA 22216, 703/276-7070.

Environmental Hazards Management Insititute, 10 Newmarket Road, P.O. Box 932, Durham, NH 03824, 603/868-1496.

Household Hazardous Waste Project, 901 South National Avenue, Box 87, Springfield,l MO 65804, 417/836-5777.

National Coalition Against the Misuse of Pesticides (NCAMP), 530 7th Street, S.W., Washington, D.C. 20003, 202/543-5450.

National Toxics Campaign, 37 Temple Place, Boston, MA 02111, 617/232-0327.

Pesticide Action Network North America Regional Center, 965 Mission Street, #514 San Francisco, CA 94103, 415/541-9140.

Recycling

Conservatree Paper Co., 10 Lombard Street, Suite 250, San Francisco, CA 94111, 415/433-1000.

Earth Care Paper Co., P.O. Box 3335 Madison, WI 53704, 608/256-5522.

Ecolo-Haul Recycling, P.O. Box 34819, Los Angeles, CA 90034, 213/838-5848.

Keep America Beautiful, Inc., 9 West Broad Street, Stamford, CT 06902, 203/323-8987.

Institute for Local Self-Reliance, 2425 18th Street, N.W., Washington, D.C. 20009, 202/232-4108.

Prairie Paper Company, 825 M St., Suite 101, Lincoln, NE 64508, 402/477-0825.

Species Extinction

The Nature Conservancy, 1815 North Lynn St., Arlington, VA 22209.

Water Pollution and Conservation

California Department of Water Resources, 1416 9th Street, P.O. Box 942836, Sacramento, CA 94236-0001, 916/445-9248.

Clean Water Action Project, 317 Pennsylvania Avenue, S.E., Washington, D.C. 20003, 202/547-1196.

Resource Conservation Inc., P.O. Box 71., Greenwich, CT 06836, 800/243-2862.

General Environmental Organizations

Council on Economic Priorities, 30 Irving Place, New York, NY 10022, 212/420-1133.

Environmental Action Foundation, 1525 New Hampshire Avenue, N.W., Washington, D.C. 20036, 202/745-4870.

Friends of the Earth, 218 D Street, S.E., Washington, D.C. 20003, 202/544-2600.

Environmental Protection Agency, Public Information Center, 401 M Street, S.W., Washington, D.C. 20460, 202/382-2080.

Global Tomorrow Coalition, 1325 G Street, N.W., Suite 915, Washington, D.C. 20005, 202/628-4016.

Green Peace USA, 1426 U Street NW, Washington, D.C. 20036, 202/462-1177.

Inform, 381 Park Avenue South, New York, NY 10060, 212/689-4040.

Izaak Walton Club, 1701 N. Ft. Myer Drive #1100, Arlington, VA 22209, 703/528-1818.

Rocky Mountain Institute, 1739 Snowmass Creek Road, Snowmass, CO 81654-9199, 303/927-3128.

Seventh Generation, 126 Intervale Road, Burlington, VT 05401, 802/862-2999.

Sierra Club, 730 Polk Street, San FRancisco, CA 94109, 415/776-2211.

United Nations Environment Programme, DC2-0803 United Nations, New York, NY 10017, 212/963-8093.

Religions, Environmental Activity, and Periodicals

Eco-Justice Working Group
> National Council of Churches, Prophetic Justice Unit, Room 572, 475 Riverside Drive, New York, NY. 10115. (Representatives from the NCC membership work with community organizations on eco-justice issues for solidarity and for their own constituency education).

Eco-Justice Project Network
> Center for Religion, Ethics and Social Policy, Anabel Taylor Hall, Cornell University, Ithaca, NY 14853. (Publishes *The Egg*: A Journal of Eco-Justice).

Interfaith Center on Corporate Responsibility
> 475 Riverside Drive, Room 566, New York, NY 10115. (Works on environmental issues through shareholder resolutions. Publishes *The Corporate Examiner*).

Interfaith Coalition on Energy
> P.O. Box 26577, Philadelphia, PA 19141, 215/635-1122. (Publishes *ICE Melter Newsletter*).

Institute in Culture and Creation Spirituality (Matthew Fox)
> Holy Names College, 3500 Mountain Blvd., Oakland, CA 94619. (Publishes *Creation* magazine).

Justice, Peace and Integrity of Creation
World Council of Churches, P.O. Box 2100, CH-1211, Geneva 2, Switzerland. (See Appendix E for publications).
Land Stewardship Project
14758 Ostlund Trail North, Marine, MN 55047. (Publishes *The Land Stewardship Letter*).
Riverdale Center of Religious Research (Thomas Berry) 5801 Palisade Ave., Riverdale, NY 10471, 212/548-1182.
The Center for Reflection on the Second Law, 8420 Camellia Dr., Raleigh, NC 27613. (Publishes *Circular*).
The Land Stewardship Council of North Carolina, Rte 4, Box 426, Pittsboro, NC 27312. (Publishes *Cry North Carolina*).
The North American Conference on Christianity and Ecology (NACCE), P.O. Box 14305, San Francisco, CA 94114. (Publishes *Firmament*).
The North American Conference on Religion and Ecology (NACRE), 5 Thomas Circle, NW, Washington, D.C. 20005. (Publishes *ECO-LETTER*).
The National Catholic Rural Life Conference, 4625 Beaver Avenue, Des Moines, IA 50310, 515/270-2634. (Publishes *Earth Matters, and Common Ground*).

Community Organizations on Environment

Alabamians for Clean Environment, 491 Country Club Road, York, AL 36925, 205/392-7443.
Citizens Alert (nuclear issues), P.O. Box 5391, Reno, NV 89513.
Citizens Clearing House for Hazardous Wastes, P.O.Box 926, Arlington, VA 22216, 703/276-7070.
Citizens for Better America, P.O. Box 356, Halifax, VA 24558. 804/476-7757.
Ecumenical Task Force of the Niagara Frontier, 259 Fourth St., Niagara Falls, NY 14303, 716/284-0026.
Highland Center, Route #3, Box 370, New Market, TN 37871, 615/933-3443.
Maine People's Alliance (Nat'l Campaign Against Toxics), R.R. 1, Box 955, Poland Springs, ME 04274, 207/926-3474.
Missourians Against Hazardous Waste, 17 Trembley Lane, Wright City, MO 63390, 314/745-3980.
National Toxic Campaign, 1168 Commonwealth Ave., Boston, MA 02134, 617/232-0327.
Southwest Organizing Project, 211 10th St., SW, Albuquerque, NM 87102, 505/247-8832.
Southwest Research and Information, P.O. Box 4524, Albuquerque, NM 87106.
West County Toxics Coalition, 1019 MacDonald Ave., Richmond, CA 94801.

APPENDIX D

ADDITIONAL RESOURCES FOR READING

Austin, Richard Cartwright.
Baptised Into Wilderness: A Christian Perspective on John Muir. John Knox Press, Atlanta. 1987.
Beauty of the Lord: Awakening the Senses. John Knox Press, Atlanta. 1988.
Hope for the Land: Nature in the Bible. John Knox Press, Atlanta. 1988.
Reclaiming America: Restoring Nature to Culture. Creekside Press, Abingdon, VA. 1990.

Berry, Thomas.
The Dreams of the Earth. Sierra Club Books. San Francisco. 1988.

Berry, Wendell.
The Unsettling of America: Culture and Agriculture. Avon, New York. 1977.
The Gift of Good Land: Further Essays Cultural and Agricultural. North Point Press. 1981.
What Are People For? North Point Press. San Francisco. 1990.

Birch, Charles and Cobb, John B. Jr.
The Liberation of Life: From the Cell to the Community. Cambridge University Press, Cambridge, England. 1981.

Brueggemann, Walter.
The Land: Place as Gift, Promise, and Challenge in Biblical Faith. Fortress Press, Philadelphia. 1977.

Commoner, Barry.
Making Peace With the Planet. Pantheon Books, New York. 1990.

DeVall, Bill and George Session.
Deep Ecology: Living As If Nature Mattered. Peregrine Smith. 1985.

Dillard, Annie.
Pilgrim at Tinker Creek. Bantam Books, New York. 1974.

Fox, Matthew.
Original Blessing. Bear & Company, Santa Fe, NM. 1983.

The Coming of the Cosmic Christ: The Healing of Mother Earth and the Birth of a Global Renaissance. Harper & Row. 1988.

Granberg-Michelson, Wesley.
A Worldly Spirituality; The Call to Redeem Life on Earth. Harper & Row, New York. 1984.

Ecology and Life: Accepting Our Environmental Responsibility. Waco, Texas. Word Book. 1988.

Tending the Garden: Essays on the Gospel and the Earth. Eerdmans. 1987. (Edited by Granberg-Michelson)

Hall, Douglas John.
Imaging God: Dominion As Stewardship. Eerdmans Publishing Co. and Friendship Press. 1986.

Hallman, David G.
Caring for Creation: The Environmental Crisis: A Canadian Christian Call to Action. Wood Lake Books. 1989.

Heilbroner, Robert L.
An Inquiry Into the Human Prospect. W. W. Norton, New York. 1974, 1980 (updated).

Hessel, Dieter, T., Ed.
For Creation's Sake: Preaching, Ecology, and Justice. General Press, Philadelphia. 1985.

Huntertmark, Nadine, Ed.
Pro-Earth: Readings on Current Land and Water Issues in the Global Environment (with Leader's Guide and Youth Leader's Guide). Friendship Press, New York. 1985.

Joranson Philip, Butigan, Ken, Ed.
Cry of the Environment: Rebuilding the Christian Creation Tradition. Bear & Company, Santa Fe, NM. 1984.

McCollough, Charles.
To Love the Earth. Office for Church and Society, United Church of Christ, 110 Maryland, Ave. NE, Washington, D.C. 20002. 1987.

McDonagh, Sean.
To Care for the Earth: A Call to a New Theology. Bear & Co. Santa Fe, NM. 1986.

McFague, Sallie.
Models of God: Theology for an Ecological, Nuclear Age. Fortress Press, Philadelphia. 1987.

Moltmann, Jurgen.
Creating a Just Future, Trinity Press International, Philadelphia. 1989.

God in Creation: A New Theology of Creation and the Spirit of God, Harper & Row. 1985.

Myers, Norman.
Gaia: An Atlas of Planet Management. Anchor Books, New York. 1984.

Owensby, Walter.
Economics for Prophets. Eerdmans. 1988.

Rowthorn, Anne.
Caring For Creation: Toward an Ethic of Responsibility. Moorehouse Publishing. 1989.

Ruether, Rosemary Radford.
Sexism and God-Talk: Toward a Feminist Theology. Beacon Press, Boston. 1983.

Santmire, H. Paul.
The Travail of Nature: The Ambiguous Ecological Promise of Christian Theology. Fortress, Philadelphia. 1985.

Sittler, Joseph.
Essays on Nature and Grace. Fortress Press, Philadelphia. 1972.

Gravity and Grace: Reflections & Provocations. Oxford-Fortress. 1986.

Soelle, Dorothee With Shirley A. Cloyes.
To Work and to Love: A Theology of Creation. Fortress Press. 1984.

Ward, Barbara and Dubos, René.
Only One Earth: The Care and Maintenance of a Small Planet. W.W. Norton, New York. 1972.

Wilkinson, Loven, Ed.
Earthkeeping: Christian Stewardship of Natural Resources. William B. Eerdmans. 1980.

Presbyterian Eco-Justice Task Force.
Keeping and Healing the Creation. Louisville, KY. 1989.

World Commission on Enviroment and Development.
Our Common Future. Oxford University Press, Oxford and New York. 1987.

World Resources 1990-91.
A Report by the World Resources Institute in Collaboration With the United Nations Environment Program and the United Nations Development Program. Oxford University Press, Oxford and New York. 1990.

APPENDIX E

WORLD COUNCIL OF CHURCHES
PUBLICATIONS
(Justice, Peace and Integrity of Creation Resources)

Duchrow, Ulrich and Liedke, Gerhard.
Shalom: Biblical Prespectives on Creation, Justice and Peace. 1989.

Niles, D. Preman.
Resisting the Threats to Life: Covenanting for Justice, Peace and Integrity of Creation. 1989.

JPIC Resource Material Kits Nos. 2, 3,4, 5, 6.

Second Draft Document for the WCC World Convocation, Seoul, Korea. March 6-12, 1990.

Order from WCC U.S. Office Publications, 475 Riverside Drive, Room 915, New York, NY 10115.

OTHER RESOURCES

"Peace With Justice," The Official Documentation of the European Ecumenical Assembly, Basel, Switzerland, 15-21 May, 1989. Published by the Conference of European Churches, P.O. Box 66, 150 route de Ferney, CH-1211 Geneva 20.

APPENDIX F

ACTION-ORIENTED
GUIDES AND RESOURCES
(First Aid for Planet Earth)

101 Ways To Help Save The Earth: With 52 Weeks of Congregational Activities to Save the Earth. United Methodist Church & Society - Environmental Justice, 100 Maryland Ave. NE, Washington, D.C. 20002, 202/488-5649.

2 Minutes a Day for a Greener Planet, Harper & Row, San Francisco. 1990.

50 Simple Things You Can Do to Save the Earth. The Earth Works Group (Box 25, 1400 Shattuck Avenue, Berkeley, CA 94709). 1990.

The Global Ecology Handbook: What You Can Do About the Environmental Crisis. The Global Tomorrow Coalition (Beacon Press). 1990.

50 Simple Things Kids Can Do to Save the Earth. The Earthworks Group (Andrews & McMeel). Solutions to Ecological problems. 1990.

Shopping for a Better World. Council on Economic Priorities (Ballantine Books). 1990.

Caplan, Ruth.
> *Our Earth, Ourselves: The Action-oriented Guide to Help You Protect and Preserve Our Environment.* Bantam Books. 1990.

Eklington, John, Hailes, Julia, and Makower, Joel.
> *The Green Consumer,* (Penguin Books). 1990.

Fritsch, Albert J., S.J.
> *Earthen Vessels: An Environmental Action Manual for Churchgoers.* P.O. Box 298, Livingston, KY 40445. 1989.

Heloise.
> *Hints for a Healthy Planet.* Putnam Publishing (200 Madison Ave., New York, NY 10016). 1990.

Hynes, Patricia H.
> *Earth Right: Every Citizen's Guide.* (Prima/St. Martin's Press). 1990.

Longacre, Doris Janzen
> *Living More With Less.* Herald Press. 1980.
>
> *More With Less Cookbook.* Herald Press. 1976.

MacEachern, Diane.
Save Our Planet: 750 Ways You Can Help Clean Up the Earth. Dell. 1990.

Null, Gary.
Cleaner, Clearer, Safer, Greener: A Blueprint for Detoxifying Your Environment. (Villard Books). 1990.

Rifkin, Jeremy, Ed.
The Green Lifestyle Handbook. Henry Holt. 1990.

Sombke, Lawrence.
The Solution to Pollution: 101 Things You Can Do to Clean Up Your Environment. Master Media, New York. 1990.

Steger, Will and Jon Bowermaster.
Saving the Earth: A Citizen's Guide to Environmental Action. Alfred A. Knopf. 1990.

APPENDIX G

Audio-visuals
(videos)

Acid Rain

What Price Clean Air? 58 min., VHS. Gives global perspective on acid rain. Documents Britain's role in Sweden's acid rain. Presents evidence of US-originated acid rain damaging Canadian environment. Shows how Japanese industries are non-polluting. Argues for a tough US Clean Air Act. Purchase or rent from Richter Productions, 330 West 42nd St., New York, NY 10036. 212/947-1395.

Asbestos

Asbestos Alert: Strategies for Safety and Health. 30 min. VHS. Presents victims of asbestos by occupations and safe ways to work with asbestos. Not anti-business. Pro-safety and pro-health. Purchase or rent from Richter Productions, 330 W. 42nd St., New York, NY 10036. 212/947-1395.

Citizen Action

The Rush to Burn. 35 min. VHS. US industries produce over 525 billion pounds of hazardous waste every year. Industries are encouraged to use incinerators to burn the waste. The video examines whether incineration is safe, whether the government is adequately regulating this process and the alternatives to toxic burning. Tells story of citizens fighting to stop incinerator use. Purchase or rent from The Video Project, 5332 College Avenue, Suite 101, Oakland, CA 94618. 415/655-9050.

Tinka's Planet. 13 min. VHS. An entertaining introduction for elementary-age children to the need for recycling. Tinka begins to collect the family's cans, bottles and newspapers, visits the recycling center where she learns how recycling can help preserve the environment. She convinces other children and then adults to take part in recycling. Purchase or rent from The video Project, 5332 College Ave., Suite 101, Oakland, CA 94618. 415/655-9050.

We Can Make A Difference. 16 min. VHS. Concerned about the environmental crisis, 12 high school students decided to make a video that would inspire other young people to save their planet. The students worked on the project for 9 months, raising all their money and interviewing hundreds of children, ages 4-18. They asked questions about pollution, global warming, ozone destruction, desertification, and most importantly, whether young people can make a difference. The video is a great discussion starter and a testimony to the power of young people. Purchase or rent from The Video Project, 5332 College Ave., Suite 101, Oakland, CA 94618. 415/655-9050.

Greenhouse Effect

Our Threatened Heritage. 19 min. VHS. Provides a concise overview of the destruction of rainforests and what can be done to stop it. The link between environment and development is also explored. Provides an excellent summary of the demise of one of our most important ecosystems. Useful for young adult and general audiences. Purchase or rent from The Video Project, 5332 College Avenue, Suite 101, Oakland, CA 94618. 415/655-9050.

Greenhouse Crisis—The American Response. 11 min. VHS. Illustrates the relationship between energy consumption, the greenhouse effect, and global warming. Based on research by the Union of Concerned Scientists, it also provides positive steps to help fight this environmental threat. Designed for general audiences. Comes with a study guide. Purchase or rent from The Video Project, 5332 College Ave., Suite 101, Oakland, CA 94618. 415/655-9050.

Can Polar Bears Tread Water? 60 min. VHS. Examines global warming caused by the burning of fossil fuels, industrial use of "greenhouse gasses," and deforestation. Purchase from Better World Society, 1100 17th St. N.W., Ste 502, Washington, D.C. 20036. 202/331-3770.

Nuclear Energy

Incident at Brown's Ferry. 57 min. VHS. Investigates nuclear energy and safety based on an accident at Brown's Ferry, Alabama, 1976. Chernobyl and Three Mile Island were not surprises after what happened at Brown's Ferry. Depicts how a nuclear power plant works, what went wrong and why. Prominent scientists articulate controversial issues surrounding nuclear energy. Purchase or rent from Richter Productions, 330 W. 42nd St., New York, NY 10036. 212/947-1395.

Nuclear Winter

Nuclear Winter: Changing Our Way of Thinking. 58 min. VHS. The use of even a fraction of the world's nuclear arsenal would have a devastating climatic consequences. Civilization as we know it would be destroyed and the human species would possibly be extinct. Dr. Carl Sagan presents the results of the research into Nuclear Winter, illustrating his talk with extensive visuals. Purchase or rent from The Video Project, 5332 College Avenue, Suite 101, Oakland, CA 94618. 415/655-9050.

Dark Circle. 60 min. VHS. A powerful examination of plutonium processing, nuclear weapons construction, and environmental contamination. Focus primarily on the Rocky Flats Processing plant in Colorado. Purchase from Better World Society, 1100 17th St. N.W., Ste 502, Washington, D.C. 20036. 202/331-3770.

Pesticides, Herbicides

A Plague on Our Children. Two parts, 58 mins. each. VHS. Part I: Dioxins and herbicides. Part II: PCBs and regulating Hazardous Waste. Tells the story of a family that had to move to escape the problems caused by pesticides. Reveals the growing evidence that dioxins and PCBs are the most dangerous and widespread contaminants on this planet. Documents the increasing politicization of Americans who have found these industrial wastes in their own backyard. Purchase or rent from Richter Productions, 330 W. 42nd St., New York, NY 10036. 212/947-1395.

For Export Only: Pesticides and Pills. Two parts, 57 minutes each. VHS. Part I: Pesticides; Part II: Pharmaceuticals. Part I documents the shocking information about US and Western Europe multinational corporations that export products prohibited or severely restricted in the countries where they are made. Ironically, the banned pesticides are used on products such as coffee and bananas that we import. Part II is about an anabolic steroid, prohibited in the US, being promoted and sold in Third World countries as an appetite stimulant. It causes irreversible sex changes in children. Purchase or rent from Richter Productions, 330 W. 42nd St., New York, NY 10036. 212/947-1395.

The Secret Agent. 57 min. Dioxin, Agent Orange, chemical warfare, agricultural herbicides. What is the truth about these substances we've used to help grow our crops at home and to defoliate jungles abroad. Documents the story of the use of defoliant code-named Agent Orange in the Vietnam War, from the Geneva Protocol of 1925 to the massive class action suit settled out of court in 1984. Purchase or rent from First Run/Icarus Films, 153 Waverly Place, New York, NY 10014. 212/243-0600.

Rainforests

Our Threatened Heritage (see listing under Greenhouse Effect).

Earth First: The Struggle for the Australian Rainforest. 58 Min. VHS. Highlights the plight of our oldest living link with the past, the majestic rainforests, and the dramatic struggle to save them. Set in Australia, the program looks at a 70 sq. kilometer stand of rainforest, which is all that remains from an age when Australia was the center of a mighty supercontinent covered by a magnificent emerald rainforest. It is also the story of a people who care and who went through extraordinary efforts to save these rainforests. Purchase or rent from The Video Project, 5332 College Ave., Suite 101, Oakland, CA 94618. 415/655-9050.

Can Polar Bears Tread Water? (see listing under Greenhouse Effect).

Environment Under Fire: Ecology and Politics in Central America. 28 min. VHS. Depicts the seriously endangered natural environment in Central America through the burning of rainforests and the use of deadly pesticides imported from the United States. Much of the land so cleared is used to export cattle and crops to the US. Explores issues and offers solutions. Purchase or rent from The Video Project, 5332 College Ave., Suite 101, Oakland, CA 94618. 415/655-9050.

Voice of the Amazon. 60 min. VHS. The story of Chico Mendes, Brazilian environmentalist and rubber tapper. The impact of his life, work, and murder is explored. His fight for the preservation of the rainforest cost him his life. Purchase from Better World Society, 1100 17th St. N.W., Ste 502, Washington, D.C. 20036. 202/331-3770.

Recycling

Tinka's Planet (see listing under Citizen Action).

Stewardship of Creation

From This Valley: On Defending the Family Farm. 20 min. VHS. Outlines the history of family farming in the USA and explains the church's decision to defend it. Emphasizes the stewardship of creation. Produced by Office of Interpretation, General Assembly Mission Board, Presbyterian Church (USA), 100 Witherspoon, Louisville,KY 40202.

Creation's Caretakers. 28 min. VHS video on the call we all share to bring justice to agriculture, environment, and rural communities. Purchase from United Methodist Board of Church and Society, 100 Maryland Avenue NE, Washington, D.C. 20002.

Sustainable Agriculture

Growing Concerns: The Future of America's Farmland. From: American Farmland Trust, 1920 N. Street, NW, Suite 400, Washington, D.C. 20036.

Watch on Washington: Sustainable Agriculture. From: Hamilton Productions, Inc. 236 Massachusetts Ave., NE, Suite 610, Washington, DC 20002.

Sustainable Agriculture. 23 min. Describes in general terms what is meant by this philosophy and the practices that are included in its implementation. From: Charles Francis, Department of Agronomy, University of Nebraska, Lincoln, NE 68583.

Toxic Waste

For Our Children: Protecting Creation From Poison. 25 min. VHS A documentary on hazardous wastes and toxic pollution depicting where the US churches are in regard to the issue of ecological justice. Focuses mainly on the "chemical corridor," where a small group called AWARE has organized in opposition to various environmental threats, including commercial incineration of hazardous waste by Dow Chemical. Comes with a 42-page study guide. Purchase for $25 from Discipleship Resources for Church and Society, P. O. Box 189, Nashville, TN 37202.

Rush to Burn (see listing under Citizen Action).

The River That Harms. 45 min. VHS. Documents the largest radioactive waste spill in US history—a national tragedy that has received little media attention. With the sound of a thunderclap, 94 million gallons of water contaminated with uranium mining waste broke through a United Nuclear Corporation storage dam in 1979. The water poured into the Puerco River in New Mexico—the main water supply for the Navajo Indians that live along the river, and a tributary of the major source of water for L.A. Navajo ranchers, their children, and farm animals waded through the river unaware of the danger. Tells the story of this tragedy and the toll it continues to take on the Navajos, who have lost the use of their water and witnessed the sickness and death of their animals. It is a prophetic warning to all humanity. Purchase or rent from The Video Project, 5332 College Ave., Suite 101, Oakland, CA 94618. 415 655-9050.

The Wipp Trail. 54 min. VHS. Tons of radioactive waste generated by the nation's nuclear weapons production facilities is being readied for cross-country travel to the first "permanent" nuclear waste disposal site, located near Carlsbad, NM. Regular nuclear shipments will pass through 28 states for the next 25 years on the way to the controversial WIPP Site (Waste Isolation Pilot Plant). The WIPP Trail video is the first program to explore the problems this waste will pose to the millions of people in communities along the transportation route and near the dump site. It also shows why citizens groups are concerned that political considerations are preventing the resolution of major health and safety issues. Purchase or rent from The Video Project, 5332 College Avenue, Suite 101, Oakland, CA 94618. 415/655-9050.

The Earth Betrayed: How the U.S. Environmental Protection Agency Protects the Poisoners—Not the People. 30 min. VHS. Reveals how the US-EPA systematically betrays the public interest by protecting industries that poison our communities. Important for those who wish to know about the real forces behind the destruction of our environment. Purchase for $29.95 plus postage from Organizing Media Project, 1844 Columbia Road, NW, Washington, DC 20009. 202/387-1000.

Other Videos

Christians for the Earth Series. Two videos: (1) Christian Ecology. 60 Min. VHS. (2) "Environmental Ethics". 30 min. Has an introduction, plus Wendell Berry in Christianity and Ecology and Wes Jackson on "Facing the Problem". Contact the North American Conference on Religion and Ecology, 5 Thomas Circle, NW, Washington, D.C. 20005.

Common Ground. 55 min. Depicts the common concerns of farmers and environmentalists. Produced by PBS and the Audubon Society. 1987. Available free from Land Stewardship Project, 512 W. Elm Street, Stillwater, MN 55082.

"The Desert Doesn't Bloom Here Anymore". 55 min documentary film or videotape produced by NOVA. 1987. Desertification in Sahel of Africa and water problems of the American West are discussed and described. Call 1-800-621-2131 for information about the video.

God and Country. 18 min. Video with study guide featuring famous environmental author Wendell Berry talking about issues the organized church faces when it takes environmental issues seriously. Thoughtful and intelligent. Order from North American Conference on Religion and Ecology, 5 Thomas Circle, N.W.,

Washington, D.C. 20005, or order from the Evangelical Lutheran Church in America, Hunger Project, 8765 West Higgins Road, Chicago, IL 60631.

Wraths of Grapes. 15 min. Shows the effects of pesticides on farm workers and their families. Describes grape Boycott. Produced by the National Farm Workers Ministry, P.O. Box 302, Delano, CA 93216. Available from United Farm Workers of America, P.O. Box 62, Keene, CA 93531.

APPENDIX H.1

Chief Seattle, leader of the Suquamish tribe in the Washington territory, delivered a prophetic speech, in 1854, to mark the transferral of ancestral Indian lands to the federal government. An adaptation of his remarks, based on an English translation by William Arrowsmith, follows.

The Great Chief in Washington sends word that he wishes to buy our land.

The Great Chief also sends us words of friendship and good will. This is kind of him, since we know he has little need of our friendship in return. But we will consider your offer. For we know that if we do not sell, the white man may come with guns and take our land.

How can you buy or sell the sky, the warmth of the land? The idea is strange to us.

If we do not own the freshness of the air and the sparkle of the water, how can you buy them?

Every part of this earth is sacred to my people. Every shining pine needle, every sandy shore, every mist in the dark woods, every clearing and humming insect is holy in the memory and experience of my people. The sap which courses through the trees carries the memories of the red man.

The white man's dead forget the country of their birth when they go to walk among the stars. Our dead never forget this beautiful earth, for it is the mother of the red man. We are part of the earth and it is part of us. The perfumed flowers are our sisters; the deer, the horse, the great eagle, these are our brothers. The rocky crests, the juices in the meadows, the body heat of the pony, and man—all belong to the same family.

So, when the Great Chief in Washington sends word that he wishes to buy our land, he asks much of us.

So, when the Great Chief sends word he will reserve us a place so that we can live comfortably to ourselves. He will be our father and we will be his children.

So we will consider your offer to buy our land. But it will not be easy. For this land is sacred to us.

This shining water that moves in the streams and rivers is not just water but the blood of our ancestors. If we sell you land, you must remember that it is sacred, and you must teach your children that it is sacred, and that each ghostly reflection in the clear water of the lake tells of events and memories in the life of my people. The water's murmur is the voice of my father's father.

The rivers are our brothers, they quench our thirst. The rivers carry our canoes, and feed our children. If we sell you our land, you must remember, and teach your children, that the rivers are our brothers, and yours, and you must henceforth give the rivers the kindness you would give any brother.

The red man has always retreated before the advancing white man, as the mist of the mountain runs before the morning sun. But the ashes of our fathers are sacred. Their graves are holy ground, and so these hills, these trees, this portion of earth is consecrated to us. We know that the white man does not understand our ways. One portion of land is the same to him as the next, for he is a stranger who comes in the night and takes from the land whatever he needs. The earth is not his brother, but his enemy, and when he has conquered it, he moves on. He leaves his father's graves behind, and he does not care. He kidnaps the earth from his children. He does not care. His father's graves and his children's birthright are forgotten. He treats his mother, the earth, and his brother, the sky as things to be bought, plundered, sold like sheep or bright beads. His appetite will devour the earth and leave behind only a desert.

I do not know. Our ways are different from your ways. The sight of your cities pains the eyes of the red man. But perhaps it is because the red man is a savage and does not understand.

There is no quiet place in the white man's cities. No place to hear the unfurling of leaves in spring or the rustle of insect's wings. But perhaps it is because I am a savage and do not understand. The clatter only seems to insult the ears. And what is there to life if a man cannot hear the lonely cry of the whippoorwill or the arguments of the frogs around a pond at night? I am a red man and do not understand. The Indian prefers the soft sound of the wind darting over the face of a pond, and the smell of the wind itself, cleansed by a midday rain, or scented with the pinon pine.

The air is precious to the red man, for all things share the same breath — the beast, the tree, the man, they all share the same breath. The white man does not seem to notice the air he breathes. Like a man dying for many days, he is numb to the stench. But if we sell you our land, you must remember that the air is precious to us, that the air shares its spirit with all the life it supports. The wind that give our grandfather his first breath also receives his last sigh. And the wind must also give our children the spirit of life. And if we sell you our land, you must keep it apart and sacred, as a place where even the white man can go to taste the wind that is sweetened by the meadow's flowers.

So we will consider your offer to buy our land. If we decide to accept, I will make one condition: The white man must treat the beasts of his land as his brothers.

I am a savage and do not understand any other way. I have seen a thousand rotting buffaloes on the prairie, left by the white man who shot them from a passing train. I am a savage and I do not understand how the smoking iron horse can be more important than the buffalo that we kill only to stay alive.

What is man without the beasts? If all the beasts were gone, men would die from a great loneliness of spirit. For whatever happens to the beasts, soon happens to man. All things are connected.

You must teach your children that the ground beneath their feet is the ashes of our grandfathers. So that they will respect the land, tell your children that the earth is rich with the lives of our kin. Teach your children what we have taught our children, that the earth is our mother. Whatever befalls the earth, befalls the sons of the earth. If men spit upon the ground they spit upon themselves.

This we know. The earth does not belong to man; man belongs to the earth. This we know. All things are connected like the blood which unites one family. All things are connected.

Whatever befalls the earth befalls the sons of the earth. Man did not weave the web of life; he is merely a strand in it. Whatever he does to the web he does to himself.

But we will consider your offer to go to the reservation you have for my people. We will live apart, and in peace. It matters little where we spend the rest of our days. Our children have seen their fathers humbled in defeat. Our warriors have felt shame, and after defeat they turn their days in idleness and contaminate their bodies with sweet foods and strong drink. It matters little where we pass the rest of our days. They are not many. A few more hours, a few more winters, and none of the children of the great tribes that once lived on this earth or that roam now in small bands in the woods will be left to mourn the graves of a people once as powerful and hopeful as yours. But why should I mourn the passing of my people? Tribes are made of men, nothing more. Men come and go, like the waves of the sea.

Even the white man, whose God walks and talks with him as friend to friend, cannot be exempt from the common destiny. We may be brothers after all; we shall see. One thing we know, which the white man may one day discover—our God is the same God. You may think now that you own him as you wish to own our land; but you cannot. He is the God of man, and his compassion is equal for the red man and the white. This earth is precious to him, and to harm the earth is to heap contempt on its Creator. The white too shall pass; perhaps sooner than all other tribes. Continue to contaminate your bed, and you will one night suffocate in your own waste.

But in your perishing you will shine brightly, fired by the strength of the God who brought you to this land and for some special purpose gave you dominion over this land and over the red man. That destiny is a mystery to us, for we do not understand when the buffalo are all slaughtered, the wild horses are tamed, the secret corners of the forest heavy with the scent of many men, and the view of the ripe hills blotted by talking wires. Where is the thicket? Gone. Where is the eagle? Gone. And what is it to say good-bye to the swift pony and the hunt? The end of living and the beginning of survival.

So we will consider your offer to buy our land. If we agree, it will be to secure the reservation you have promised. There, perhaps, we may live out our brief days as we wish. When the last red man has vanished from this earth, and his memory is only the shadow of a cloud moving across the prairie, these shores and forests will still hold the spirits of my people. For they love this earth as the newborn loves its mother's heartbeat. So if we sell you our land, love it as we've loved it. Care for it as we've cared for it. Hold in your mind the memory of the land as it is when you take it. And with all your strength, with all your mind, and with all your heart, preserve it for your children, and love it...as God loves us all.

One thing we know. Our God is the same God. This earth is precious to him. Even the white man cannot be exempt from the common destiny. We may be brothers after all. We shall see.

APPENDIX H.2

THE VALDEZ PRINCIPLES

On September 7, 1989, a coalition of pension funds, church groups, environmental organizations and social investment analysts launched a new program to defend the environment— the Valdez Principles. Named for the tragic Exxon tanker Valdez, the Principles set forth ten goals for corporate behavior. They call on corporations to measure their profits only after adding up all costs of doing business, not simply financial.

The Principles originated with the Coalition for Environmentally Responsible Economies (CERES) complete, which includes the controllers of New York City, New York State and the State of California; Interfaith Center on Corporate Responsibility; National Audubon Society, National Wildlife Federation; Co-op America; Counsel on Economic Priorities; Franklin Research & Development, Calvert Social Investment Fund and many others. CERES is a project of the Social Investment Forum, an association of 325 investment professionals.

Statement of Intent

With these Principles, the Coalition for Environmentally Responsible Economies, the CERES Project of the Social Investment Forum, sets forth broad standards for evaluating activities by corporations that directly or indirectly impact the Earth's biosphere. The CERES Project has created the Valdez Principles to help investors make informed decisions around environmental issues. As representatives of the investment and environmental communities, we are asking corporations to join with us by subscribing to these Principles.

Recognizing the complexity of the issues contained in these broad Principles, CERES has attempted to define the Principles as a long term process rather than a static statement. CERES members hope that signatory companies will work with us on the elaboration of the specific requirements of these Principles. Our intent is to create a voluntary mechanism of corporate self-governance that will maintain business practices consistent with the goals of sustaining our fragile environment for future generations within a culture that respects all life and honors its interdependence.

We ask for a long term commitment to the process of compliance with these Principles and an additional commitment of assistance and cooperation in the further development of specific standards derived from each of these general principles.

Introduction

By adopting these Principles, we publicly affirm our belief that corporations and their shareholders have a direct responsibility for the environment. We believe that corporations must conduct their business as responsible stewards of the environment and seek profits only in a manner that leaves the Earth healthy and safe. We believe that corporations must not compromise the ability of future generations to sustain their needs.

We recognize this to be a long term commitment to update our practices continually in light of advances in technology and new understandings in health and environmental science. We intend to make consistent, measurable progress in implementing these Principles and to apply them wherever we operate throughout the world.

1. **Protection of the Biosphere:** We will minimize and seek to eliminate the release of pollutants that cause damage to the air, water or Earth or its inhabitants. We will safeguard habitats in rivers, lakes, wetlands, coastal zones and oceans and minimize contributing to the greenhouse effect, depletion of the ozone layer, acid rain or smog.

2. **Sustainable Use of Natural Resources:** We will make sustainable use of renewable resources, such as water, soils and forests. We will conserve nonrenewable natural resources through efficient use and careful planning. We will protect wildlife habitat, open spaces and wilderness, while preserving biodiversity.

3. **Reduction and Disposal of Wastes:** We will minimize the creation of waste, especially hazardous waste, and wherever possible recycle materials. We will dispose of waste through safe and responsible methods.

4. **Wise Use of Energy:** We will make every effort to use environmentally safe and sustainable energy sources to meet our needs. We will invest in improved energy efficiency and conservation in our operations. We will maximize energy efficiency of products we produce and sell.

5. **Risk Reduction:** We will minimize environmental, health, and safety risks to employees and communities in which we operate by employing safe technologies and operating procedures and by being constantly prepared for emergencies.

6. **Marketing of Safe Products and Services:** We will sell products or services that minimize environmental impacts and are

safe as consumers use them. We will inform consumers of environmental impacts of products or services.

7. Damage Compensation: We will take responsibility for harm we cause to the environment by making every effort to fully restore the environment and to compensate persons adversely affected.

8. Disclosure: We will disclose to employees and to the public incidents relating to operations that cause environmental harm or pose health and safety hazards. We will disclose potential environmental, health or safety hazards posed by operations and take no action against employees who report conditions that create a danger to the environment or pose health and safety hazards.

9. Environmental Directors and Managers: At least one member of the Board of Directors will be a person qualified to represent environmental interests. We will commit management resources to implement these Principles, including funding an office of vice-president for environmental affairs or an equivalent executive position, reporting directly to the CEO, to monitor and report upon implementation efforts.

10. Assessment and Annual Audit: We will conduct and make public an annual self-evaluation of progress in implementing these Principles and in complying with all applicable laws and regulations throughout worldwide operations. We will work toward the timely creation of independent environmental audit procedures completed annually and made available to the public.

For additional information contact: Coalition for Environmentally Responsible Economics, 711 Atlantic Avenue, Boston, MA 02111, 617/451-0927.